PLANTS IN PLACE

CRITICAL LIFE STUDIES

CRITICAL LIFE STUDIES

JAMI WEINSTEIN, CLAIRE COLEBROOK, AND MYRA J. HIRD, SERIES EDITORS

The core concept of critical life studies strikes at the heart of the dilemma that contemporary critical theory has been circling around: namely, the negotiation of the human, its residues, a priori configurations, the persistence of humanism in structures of thought, and the figure of life as a constitutive focus for ethical, political, ontological, and epistemological questions. Despite attempts to move quickly through humanism (and organicism) to more adequate theoretical concepts, such haste has impeded the analysis of how the humanist concept of life is preconfigured or immanent to the supposedly new conceptual leap. The Critical Life Studies series thus aims to destabilize critical theory's central figure, life—no longer should we rely upon it as the horizon of all constitutive meaning but instead begin with life as the problematic of critical theory and its reconceptualization as the condition of possibility for thought. By reframing the notion of life critically—outside the orbit and primacy of the human and subversive to its organic forms—the series aims to foster a more expansive, less parochial engagement with critical theory.

Paul B. Preciado, *Countersexual Manifesto* (2019)

Vincent Bruyere, *Perishability Fatigue: Forays Into Environmental Loss and Decay* (2018)

Penelope Deutscher, *Foucault's Futures: A Critique of Reproductive Reason* (2017)

Jami Weinstein and Claire Colebrook, eds., *Posthumous Life: Theorizing Beyond the Posthuman* (2017)

Luce Irigaray and Michael Marder, *Through Vegetal Being: Two Philosophical Perspectives* (2016)

PLANTS IN PLACE

A PHENOMENOLOGY OF THE VEGETAL

EDWARD S. CASEY AND MICHAEL MARDER

Columbia University Press   *New York*

Columbia University Press
Publishers Since 1893
New York   Chichester, West Sussex
cup.columbia.edu

Copyright © 2024 Columbia University Press
All rights reserved

Library of Congress Cataloging-in-Publication Data
Names: Casey, Edward S., 1939– author. | Marder, Michael, 1980– author.
Title: Plants in place : a phenomenology of the vegetal /
Edward S. Casey and Michael Marder.
Description: New York : Columbia University Press, [2023] |
Series: Critical life studies | Includes bibliographical references and index.
Identifiers: LCCN 2023021835 (print) | LCCN 2023021836 (ebook) |
ISBN 9780231213448 (hardback) | ISBN 9780231213455 (trade paperback) |
ISBN 9780231559898 (ebook)
Subjects: LCSH: Plants (Philosophy)
Classification: LCC B105.P535 C37 2023 (print) | LCC B105.P535 (ebook) |
DDC 113/.8—dc23/eng/20230811
LC record available at https://lccn.loc.gov/2023021835
LC ebook record available at https://lccn.loc.gov/2023021836

Printed and bound by CPI Group (UK) Ltd, Croydon, CR0 4YY

Cover design: Julia Kushnirsky
Cover painting: Edward S. Casey

CONTENTS

Preface: Walking Among Plants vii
Acknowledgments xxv

1 The Placial Basis of Plant Sessility and Mobility   1

2 Peripheral Power: Structural Dynamics at the Edges of Plants   17

Interlude 1 How Plants Think   39

3. Taking Trees Over the Edge   47

Interlude 2 Plants Up-Close: The Case of Moss   71

4 The Shared Sociality of Trees, with Implications for Place   81

Interlude 3 Plants from Afar: As Seen in Landscape Painting   105

5 Attachment and Detachment in the Place of Plants   119

Conclusion: The Fate of Places, the Fate of Plants   139

Notes 159
Index 171

PREFACE
Walking Among Plants

When we walk, we naturally go to the fields and woods: what would become of us, if we walked only in a garden or a mall?
—Thoreau, "Walking"

I who lose myself like an insect among the grasses of the meadow . . . I barely dare to hope to herborize as well as the sheep which pass under my window.
—Rousseau, "Letter to the Duchess of Portland"

I

On the verge of a journey we shall be sharing with you, and as we get ready to undertake an experiment in phyto-peripatetics, let us begin with a simple contrast. When we walk in a field, meander in a grove, or stroll in a garden, we move among plants that stay in place. It bears noting right away that the contrast is a little deceptive: vegetal being-in-place is not the opposite of movement. Plants move in the locales of their growth by virtue of growing, irradiating outward, unfurling themselves, and experiencing a lived time-space that does not predate them as an empty continuum and that coevolves together with and as them. Even so, human displacement among trees, shrubs, grasses, and flowers accentuates our locomotion against the backdrop of their presumably stationary existence. And this bare beginning, discernible in the contrast, which will accompany us all the way to the end, has ramifications in diverse domains.

The most unsympathetic interpretation would assert that, playing with the opposition between human mobility and vegetal immobility, we (however unconsciously) establish or reestablish our superiority over the flora. It is as though walkers are saying by means of their bodies' kinetic activity and, hence, without uttering anything: "Look: I can linger for a little while in the shade of an oak or in front of a rose, but I can also move on, whether to another plant or to another place altogether. Or I might not linger at all, rather keeping a steady pace at which the vegetation around me coalesces into a kind of green blur. In these possibilities, reflecting my decision, lies my freedom—the freedom you, plants, cannot have." We reject this cruel interpretation, especially in those cases when walking among plants is done for nothing, i.e., not in order to reach some other destination but to lose and perhaps discover (or rediscover) oneself in the vegetal world.

As we walk among plants, the self-dislocating movement we practice intersects with the emplaced varieties of movement in which plants excel. The fact that trees, bushes, flowers, and grass we tread upon, walk under, or navigate in between stay put can only appear as a privation from the standpoint of an exclusive focus on locomotion, which does not, by far, exhaust all the rich senses of movement. We propose an interpretation that is the opposite of attributing privation or lack to plants: walking among them, we—this "we" constructed together with plants—piece together all the possible varieties of movement in a dynamic situation, where neither of the participants, whether vegetal or human, embodies movement as such. At the same time, growth, decay, and to a lesser extent (and, perhaps, provoking more worries and concerns), metamorphosis also obtain for movements of our living cells and tissues. They are, nonetheless, usually too subtle and slow for us to notice them. Walking among plants is, in this sense, both responding to the irresistible call of vegetal places and being recalled to ourselves, to the uncanny features, both intimately close and utterly foreign, of our corporeity and psychic life.

II

We walk among plants whenever and wherever we walk—in the country, in the city, in the suburbs: virtually everywhere, except for the most barren desert, certain urban areas devoid of trees, or the empty roof of a tall building. In walking outside our homes, we find ourselves in the midst of plant life of various kinds. Gardens are an especially concentrated form of this immersion—one that can be highly structured, as in the formal garden at Versailles, and dependent on cultural models of what constitutes a garden and how it is composed (compare the centrality of the peculiarly yet naturally shaped rocks in Chinese or Japanese to British gardens, for instance). But informal gardens are no less plant-bound: indeed, they are still more so because of the density of vegetal life to be found there. In their case, not only are we surrounded by plants but also immersed in them, encouraged to lose ourselves in their midst.

Descriptively regarded, plants are punctuations in the environing landscape: clusters or bundles of living matter, both at a visual level and in terms of what we feel under our feet or up against our legs as we perambulate. But plants are much more than visual or haptic events in our lives. They are the decentered centers of vegetative energy, out from which radiates a special aura exuded by plants alone. This green aura is in part what draws us to join the company of plants by walking among them. Once walking in the free and open manner advocated by Henry David Thoreau or, in a profoundly nonanthropocentric way, by Jean-Jacques Rousseau, it matters that we are ourselves in motion and not stopping and staring at plants as isolated determinate entities, one at a time, tempting as this may be at certain moments, say for amateur botanists.[1] Our flow joins theirs; we take them in as we move, propelled forward by their subtle animation, which courses through the environment behind and in front of us, and, truth be told, on all sides. (Much the same is true of birds, who fly rather than walk among plants, seeking ways to alight on branches rather than to sit or stroll on the underlying ground, to which they may be also drawn by the seeds that have fallen there.)

Despite their many collusions, one difference between humans and plants is especially telling. While human beings walk among plants as a matter of course, plants do not, with very rare exceptions, ambulate at all. Sessile beings that they are, they *stay put*. This is so even if at a subtle level (at their root tips) they are active in extending themselves, communicating messages to other plants, and forming communities with microscopic fungal and bacterial coinhabitants of the soil.[2] This invisible activity is immense and complex, but it does not constitute *walking* by any stretch of the imagination.[3]

Humans and many other animals seek ambulation from the very start. If they cannot walk at first, they find the means to do so unless physically impaired in ways that keep them motionless. (And even then, thanks to devices such as wheelchairs, they seek to *move around* as soon as they can and as much as they can.) It is not only that human beings have an addiction to speed—most notably in the modern era, as is argued in recent books with titles such as *Speed and Politics* and *Speed Limits*—but they are supremely uncomfortable when not allowed to move, finding it virtually intolerable. When human beings are deprived of the possibility of walking, they are denied open access to plant life. As has been shown in patients hospitalized with severe illness, the sheer presence of plants is curative, so their absence can be a critical loss to human beings who are prevented from seeing them, albeit through a hospital window.[4] It is not their visual presentation alone that matters most, but the freedom to move among them at one's own leisure: to *walk in their midst*, especially if this walking is undertaken freely and can range fairly broadly. Such walking can occur by active imagination or by actual ambulation, but it is the latter that we most often seek and find most satisfying.

III

Backtracking for a moment, let us retrace our steps and comment upon peripatetic philosophy, as alive in Aristotle's Lyceum as in Rousseau's reveries. *Peri + patein:* walking around. Around what? Which perimeter does a walker-thinker circumscribe? Itinerant philosophers may well walk among plants—or the colonnades in the academy of Athens that have supplanted plants as artificial reinventions of tree trunks—but even if not, they invariably encircle themselves in their deliberations. In fact, the adjective *peripatetic* makes no mention whatsoever of the context wherein walking around takes place, and it is this abstraction from the surroundings that invisibly prepares the ground for an abstract universality indifferent to *when* and *where*. Such universality then passes for thought.

That said, the peripatetics realized, if only implicitly, that there is no direct route to oneself. Thought is activated thanks to detours and digressions—not least among them, those taken through physical walks that prompt the body to move so as to shake cognition out of its stagnation. In such walks, plants, as well as their remainders or reminders, become signposts for movement, helping to orient us in space and, above all, orienting us in thought (as in Immanuel Kant's "What Is Orientation in Thinking?"), gently guiding us, who walk among them, back to ourselves. Do they give something indispensable to thought—to thinking as an activity and its own outcome: to be pursued, thoughtfully, into the future—that cannot be found elsewhere?

Rousseau's peripatetic experience is crucially dissimilar to the one we encounter in classical philosophy. His returns to himself as thinker via the mediation of walking among plants are incidental; what prevails in his *Reveries* is the daydream, a freely associative, hardly self-conscious existence with and in the flora. His "botanical expeditions," the countryside strolls during which he collected the commonest of plant specimens, were intended to lose, rather than to find, himself. The ecstasy of the desired self-abandon was best achieved through the walker's contact with vegetation outside him, which drew him back to the vegetal dimension of his own life. For Rousseau, botany was what he called a "salutary science": a poison and a remedy, despite the pitfalls of scientific rationality, it held the potential for reorienting modern humanity away from the excesses of civilization that, more and more, had set us adrift.[5] Along the same lines, it is possible to conclude that walking among plants is conducive to a salutary movement of thought, pulling against the cognitive tendency toward abstraction and thus embedding our ideas once again in sensuous experience.

The sensuous experience of the vegetal world reawakens in us another kind of thinking resistant to abstract and decontextualized thought. Swathed in the sights and smells, tastes (if we are lucky enough to stumble upon berries or fruit) and tactile sensations (for instance, of grass against bare feet, but most often not those mediated by the hand, unless this typically privileged organ of touch is used gently to move aside a branch blocking the path), peripatetic explorers feel-think on the periphery of their sentient bodies, akin to plants that cognize the world on the outer edges of their extension (at the root tips, unfurling leaves, meristems promising future growth, etc). Rather than objectifying, thinking *of* something, or visually representing, we discover what it means to think around while walking around— peripatetically, peripherally, perimetrically. In addition to the sensuous materiality of thought, whither plants lead us, they give us this other mode of thinking to think, the mode one of us (MM) has termed "essentially superficial" and the other (EC) calls "periphenomenological." Our contact with plants could not be more literally superficial than when we walk among—not just past—them, the lived times and spaces of vegetal and human beings hardly brushing upon one another, which is what a genuine encounter between these two orders of existence looks and feels like.

IV

Gary Snyder claims that walking is "the exact balance of spirit and humility."[6] Such equipoise is the basis for free walking—a walking that is undertaken paradigmatically among plants, with which human beings have a kind of "natural contract" in Rousseau's telling expression. This contract is enacted daily in the bare but essential act of walking in places that support living beings and invite their exploration. For Snyder, walking in wilderness is "the great adventure";[7] but just where we walk meaningfully is quite variable. Walking in the simplest setting will do: in one's own side yard or around the block on which one lives. What matters most is not the sheer ambulation, good as this may be for one's health; it is walking in *natural places*: natural enough to support a few plants, if only in the form of leaves of grass.

There is, then, a natural affinity between plants and walking. Each fits the other, indeed complements the other. Walking in and with plants is walking in a setting that calls for walking and that is an intimate match for it. It is a paradigm case of *walking in place*—where "place" is not just a stretch of space but a lively presence that, more than a mere setting for moving one's feet, provides a unique dynamism that this book aims at setting forth more explicitly than has been done previously in philosophy. For we walk *from place to place* and are never not in place when walking, even if the place itself changes character as we walk—and we with it. We walk not so much *on* or *over* places as *with* them, and in so doing our being-in-the-world is altered, however subtly.

Plants, too, grow, decay, and metamorphose both in and with the places they inhabit. These are all movements, as we have already mentioned and as Aristotle had recognized in his *Physics*, even though they do not involve locomotion. The timescales of the contraction undergone in decay or extension resulting from growth are vastly different from what is perceptible from the human point of view, which is why plants are usually considered to be immobile, unmoving physically and cognitively. But this doesn't mean that subtle vegetal movements are nonexistent and, moreover, that they do not affect the places within which they move. If so, then our walking in places where plants grow is walking with places and plants in more ways than those presupposed by a momentary copresence. Walking in and with the places that support and are supported by plants is delivering our perambulating bodies and minds to the movements of plants in and with their places, movements that are ongoing and that involve *us*, if only temporarily, in their unfolding before our senses.

V

Between place and walking there is what Mary Watkins calls "mutual accompaniment."[8] By this is meant that place and walking not only fit together but that each activates what is most lively in the other. Not only does each *need* the other—place offering *somewhere* to walk and walking releasing vibrant powers inherent in the place where we walk—but each allows the other to come into its own in new and often unanticipatable ways. They form a dynamic duo—a body/place alliance that can be considered a version of what Plato designated as "the indefinite dyad."

Plants figure importantly in the intimacy of such a dyad, even if their own movements remain largely foreclosed to their being registered "in real time" by human perception. (Let us note, in passing, that this excess of what cannot be straightforwardly measured is not debilitating, but, on the contrary, stimulating, as far as the continuation of activity is concerned.) Plants populate places in two directions at once: downward into the ground by their subterranean root systems, upward into the air into which they branch and bloom. Their bipolarity (to which we shall return), rather than being alienating or divisive, establishes an axis that connects rather than separates. It connects *in place*—in the very place through which humans and other animals locomote horizontally when they walk or otherwise move in the presence of plants.

If, as Snyder maintains, "the world is places,"[9] these places are preeminently places for walking amid natural beings such as plants. As Snyder adds, "each place is its own place, forever (eventually) wild . . . the land is all small places."[10] Sometimes, the places of plants, such as a thick forest or a jungle, are too dense or inaccessible to admit human beings into them. But often the places of plants, which we can share with them, are just big enough to walk in and through, wending one's way through vegetation furnished by variegated plant life, ranging from the grass under one's feet to trees overhead. We are always between places *and* between plants clinging to the earth below and arching up above us. This is a double betweenness that is always shifting in its composition, as we move through it when walking beyond the confines of our familiar home-place and as it, itself, often moves in ways our perception cannot discern.

VI

Being on public transportation brings about a very different situation than that which characterizes walking on open ground. Highways and railroads are characteristically cleared of all plant life, though trains actually help spread pollen and seeds, stimulating the growth of biodiverse vegetation along the tracks. Moreover, while on public transit, we rarely experience the plant world up close. If it figures into our experiential domain at all, it comes to us at a distance—as when we admire a faraway vista populated by groves of trees—and it tends to slip out of sight too quickly to appreciate its many details, becoming converted into something of a green blur.[11] It emerges in and just as suddenly disappears from our field of vision rather than in the path of our walking. This reflects the fact that, instead of moving ourselves as in walking, we are *being moved* by trains or planes on which we ride: we move at their speed. As passengers, we allow ourselves to be *carried along*, whether on rails or by airplane wings. We are *passengers* in such situations, rather than active *travelers* who move through the world on our own terms, carrying ourselves along rather than being carried along.

The difference between travelers and passengers is profound. Whereas travelers are attuned to the world through which they move, "for passengers, existence is split roughly between the outside world and the inner domain."[12] If plants are noticed at all, they are *out there* in the landscape through which we are being transported—on the other side of the glass window of the automobile or train through which we look—instead of being *right here* underfoot, at one's side, or directly over us. Where the walker is ipso facto in their midst, the passenger finds herself moving *around* them, gliding beyond their living and lived presence: *escorted elsewhere* to a destination that is typically a congeries of streets and sidewalks and buildings with little if any plant life present to greet her.

While in transit, the passenger is strongly tempted to retreat to her or his "inner domain" after a few glances at the "outside world" seen on the other side of the window. The retreat is typically to rumination, a nap, or a book one is reading. It is a matter of self-absorption rather than exposure to a world where one walks by one's own energy and efforts. There is, after all, no significant walking inside a car, train, or plane, and there are few if any plants to be found in these antiseptic aherbal enclosures. The passenger is in a contemporary equivalent of René Descartes's retreat—in flight from the world of living things. While on a train or plane, we experience the contemporary equivalent of a move to *res cogitans* and away from *res extensa:* where extended things include other living beings directly encountered—as happens on the least afternoon walk, whether that of Thoreau walking west out of Concord, Rousseau wandering in the French countryside, or oneself strolling in one's local neighborhood.

If we move from a Cartesian model of being inside—inside the mind as a cognitive parallel to being inside a transport vehicle: in both cases, cut off from the environing world—to the very different Hegelian model of the dialectical relation between the *here* and the *there*, we are no longer constrained by a divisively dyadic choice. For the *here* and the *there* on G. W. F. Hegel's reading can switch positions easily and in certain situations do so continually. In his paradigmatic example, what was just *here* before me becomes *there* as I pass it by and take up a position just beyond it. But the *here* still resonates in the *there* (and in me as well), and similarly the *there* is already adumbrated in the *here* even as I am immersed in it directly.

If we stay with this dialectical direction, we are not forced to contrast being a passenger with being a walker so starkly as we are tempted to do on first consideration. We need not get off the train and start walking outside to take in the world of plants; this latter world can ingress into myself as passenger by way of a persistent memory, an eloquent poem, or my own ruminations—especially if these modalities engage in an environmental direction that brings plants into active presence. In effect, I bring the outside inside. I may still be sitting on the train, but some significant part of me is also outside the train—*out there* while also *in here*. Or rather, out-there has come in-here: has become in-herent in my thinking. By the same token, when I am outside—when the *there* has become my *here*—I can incorporate into my ongoing experience the very thoughts I was having on the train before I stepped off it, retaining these thoughts as lively presences and not merely as pallid memories. Then I bring the inside outside.

The larger lesson here is that we cannot once and for all keep directly experiencing the world of plants by walking in it altogether distinct from being stationary on a conveyance that takes us through this world in a literal separation from it. Tempting as is the Cartesian paradigm of the alienation of what we think and feel from what we experience in the world in which we walk, each implicates the other: the *there* insinuates itself into the *here*, and the *here* is already nascent in the *there*. (And this is not even to mention as of yet the *here* of each plant, which partially overlaps with our *here* both as we walk among them and as we reminisce about such experiences.) The great adventure of walking in the world of plants cannot be disconnected entirely from the inner adventure of considering this world and letting it enter into our thinking as a transmuted presence. It is a matter of "thinking in transit."[13] The world of plants is both within and without—out there where we walk in it and in here when I project or remember it. The scope of what we entertain mentally is not restricted to the limited perimeters of *res cogitans* but reaches out to touch the world in which we walk, bringing its *there* into our *here*. The plants we encounter out walking are also within us—right *here*—just as the plants within our mind and memory are also without us: out *there*.

VII

Some, including one of the authors (MM), enjoy jogging among plants: in groves, fields, along riverbanks covered in lush vegetation, or in other such places. Both speed-wise and with respect to the joggers' relation to the flora, they find themselves right in the middle between a walker and a passenger—the middle not referring to the mathematical average or mean between the speeds of walking and riding on a train, for instance, but to the experience of passing by plants. For a jogger, plants are neither as individuated as they are for a walker nor are they as deindividuated as they are for a train rider. Running on a trail among plants puts us in touch with the sense of being in the middle, in the midst of the vegetal milieu, which is itself performing a middling, spanning activity between the subterranean labyrinths below and the aerial expanses above, as well as among species and biological kingdoms.

Joggers respond in earnest to the walkers' imperative to keep moving along and not stopping, unless they need to catch their breath for a while. Consequently, they are even more prone than walkers to forego in the course of their activity a relation to plants as isolated determinate entities. This presumed loss is, however, more than compensated for by the access gained to the experience of being in the middle—itself facilitated by the middle speed and midrange relation to plants—which is, to a certain degree, shared with the vegetal world. While it is crucial to hone an ethical—singular and singularizing—approach to plants, it is equally urgent to go beyond the distinction between the particular and the universal with regard to them, not least out of respect for their peculiar mode of being. The middle distance and the middle speed of running calibrates this practice well.

PREFACE ❧ xxi

Figure 0.1. Monsanto pine forest, Lisbon, Portugal. Photograph on site by M. Marder, September 20, 2022.

As anyone who has jogged in a forest knows, doing so is energizing well beyond the release of adrenaline triggered by intense physical activity. When running atop a soft carpet of pine needles, the branches of pine trees stretching overhead, I feel dynamically supported by vegetal life in the midst of which I am moving. While a thick cover of pine needles softens the impact of jogging on knee joints, the respiration and the smell of resin emanating from these trees adds an atmospheric impetus to my perseverance and continuation of this activity. It is enough to open my chest to the crisp aroma of pines to get a second wind, my second breath, which is actually a breath "before" the first. Whether or not this approach is instrumentalizing toward plants depends on the jogger's (or the walker's, for that matter) attitude: a relation to vegetal life as a means or, conversely, as a milieu. Does one perceive oneself as an active subject, who engages a more or less impassive object, or as one among the many synergic ties that make the places of plants what they are?

VIII

Walking in the midst of plants, we above all cherish the difference between us and them, as well as the differences among them and among ourselves. Biodiversity is the diversity of *bios*—not only within any single kind of living being but also among forms of life, including the human. Smelling and seeing and touching, remembering, anticipating, and directly experiencing plants in the course of our walks, we are with plants and with the places they inhabit. And this "with," while signaling a certain proximity and intimacy of engagement, marks a minimal distance, without which there would have been nothing but an undifferentiated fusion not amounting to an experience. The frame of a stroll as signified by this "with" may recede from our minds as we are walking among, above, and under plants, but it is still there, shaping much of what is going on between us.

We thus resist the contemporary proposals, many of them inspired by the work of Gilles Deleuze and Félix Guattari, to become-X: here, to become-plant. Mature humanity, ready to share in difference with human and nonhuman beings alike, eschews the ancient mimetic need to become the other, the need betokening more than anything a certain anthropocentric imperialism. The rhythm of our walking and living among plants will never coincide with the rhythms, tempos, or temporalities of vegetal vitality, its movements virtually imperceptible because much slower than those of our locomotion. There is nothing wrong with the dissonance between the cadences of human and plant existences, revealed in the course of phyto-peripatetic ventures. The discrepancy dispenses to each their own while putting each in touch with the other: it makes us alive to the otherwise taken-for-granted pace and place of our being-in-the-world and to the underappreciated otherness of plants who are in the world in a distinct manner. Tangentially, peripherally, the act of walking among plants gives an intimation of ontological justice, appropriating neither side to the needs of the other, acknowledging the coinvolvement and mindful of the divide between the vegetal and the human.

ACKNOWLEDGMENTS

I thank the teachers who encouraged my early work in phenomenology: in the United States, George Schrader, Richard Bernstein, William Earle, James Edie; and in France, Mikel Dufrenne, Paul Ricoeur, and Jacques Derrida. Each in his own way supported the pursuit of phenomenology in many diverse directions. I suspect that they would have been delighted at the turn I take in *Plants in Place*, even though none of them ever took up this topic. It was Michael Marder who drew me into an engagement with the neglected question of the place of plants. He has been an inspiring and altogether supportive coauthor throughout our collaboration, and I wish to give him major credit for suggesting the topic of this book and pursuing it with me at every stage. Special thanks go to Wendy Lochner, publisher, philosophy and religion, at Columbia University Press, for supporting our joint project from the beginning, and to Susan Pensak for her excellent editing.

ESC

I join Ed Casey in extending my gratitude to everyone he has mentioned in his own acknowledgements. I am also grateful to GAIT, the Basque Government research group on "Social change, emerging forms of subjectivity and identity in contemporary societies" (IT1469–22), for the financial support it has provided for this project.

At the same time, if all thinking is, in a significant if poorly articulated way, a thanking, I wish to thank those who have taught and who continue to teach me how to think. Sincerest thanks go to Ed Casey himself, my very first teacher of philosophy at the New School for Social Research in New York nearly twenty years ago and now a wonderful coauthor and friend. I thank, too, the plant world, an inexhaustible source of inspiration for thinking: the old birch and date palm trees, the mosses and the tulip bulbs, a linen seed and pine forest. In every respect, plants are my teachers, and it is my hope that this book will contribute, however modestly, to cherishing and enriching the places where they grow.

MM

PLANTS IN PLACE

1

THE PLACIAL BASIS OF PLANT SESSILITY AND MOBILITY

I

What would it be like to be stuck in one place indefinitely? You can be sure that this would be supremely frustrating. Certainly so for human beings and for other animals whose lives are built on the real possibility of movement understood as displacement or relocation from one place to another. When that movement is denied, inherently mobile beings are undermined in their plans and projects. Their horizons narrow down very abruptly and drastically. If momentary only, this is bearable. But when it is a matter of being trapped in one location, it can be intolerable. Hence the extreme suffering of being held in solitary confinement in a prison—a situation that is known to lead to psychosis and suicide and, even short of these, to a form of misery unlike any other. Only the most stalwart can survive in these circumstances: Nelson Mandela, for example, who not only managed to stay sane but to do significant writing while in that altogether confined state. But this was quite exceptional. Far from flourishing, most humans regress and degenerate in such isolation—physically, psychically, socially.[1]

To be so inherently sessile suits mainly one kind of life on earth: that of plants.[2] With rare exceptions, their entire life is spent linked to one place. They not only survive there; they *flourish* in that place and in many respects make it what it is. But what does "place" mean here? Normally, we think of place as *location*: that is, a point in space or a stretch of it, in any case a unit of space—where space is considered endless, *infinite* in the word that Isaac Newton insisted on. It follows that place so conceived is something that is properly *measured* (in so many units as determined by the needs of various human projects) and *occupied* (filled up by discrete bodies), as well as essentially *measurable* and *occupiable*. But further reflection tells us that place—place *as experienced*—is something else beyond "simple location" (in Alfred North Whitehead's term for pinpointed position in space). This something else has preoccupied one of us (EC) for several decades. Here we extend these earlier reflections to the life of plants.

A leading question is this: what would it be like to be altogether stationary for a lifetime and not just for limited stretches? It is one of the major aims of this book to explore just this question. A preliminary assessment turns up the following five basic traits of plant life, all closely related with their sessile state of being:

> *burrowing action*: the roots of plants find their way through the soil, inching through the earth as in their proper element, searching for adequate nutrition; though plants have no shovels, they do find their way in the soil, as if "tunneling" through the earth and excavating it; in various scientific studies, plant roots have been found to navigate underground labyrinths (which they in part create by their burrowing actions) full of obstacles, narrow channels, and desired

resources no less effectively than animals in analogous aboveground labyrinthine settings.

downward movement: the tunneling is done in a largely *downward* direction: down from the midportion of the seed and from upper parts of plants that seek air and sun in the open air; this downward direction is an integral part of a definite trajectory, depending on the kind of plant and the geophysical region in which it is found; proceeding mainly underground, obeying the force of gravity translated into biochemical signals that tell plants where "down" is, they dig into a seemingly ever-receptive earth.

upward movement: although it is tempting to think of plants as hugging the earth from which they spring, they are also notable for their growing *up* in a vertical direction—up into the air that surrounds them and that is enriched with the oxygen they exhale as well as the moisture, which they channel from underground sources and release through their leaves, as if they are reaching into a surrounding atmosphere: their upper ambience as it were.

outward unfolding: plants grow aslant as well as down; they *branch out*; they reach out to their lateral peripheries, seeming to grasp at what surrounds them, whether this is underground or altogether aboveground; the factor of the periphery is a key here: plants grow *out around themselves* by relying on their exquisitely refined sense of proprioception.

intercalation with other life: plants, as we shall see in more detail, are inherently social beings, relating both to other plants and to other forms of life, including many beings who live largely underground (worms, various insects, and, at a microlevel, fungi and bacteria); indeed, entire communities are almost always at play in the life of plants; to be sessile is not necessarily to be solitary but may implicate an entire world of beings gathering around an "anchored" existence, some of them animate, though many are not; it should be also mentioned with regard to intercalation that the unfolding, growing, and all other vegetal movements are oriented, directed toward, or at the very least seek solar energy, moisture, and minerals, such that their symbiotic quest amounts to a coorientation, codirectedness, or vegetal cointentionality.

What at first looks like sheer passivity on the part of plants is, on closer inspection, something quite *vibrant*—a matter of *process* rather than of fixed substance. To be sessile is not to be fixed in place but to be active in place and with place. Or better yet, it is to *enact place*. It is not just to be *active in place* but to *activate place itself*, to be situated in such a way as to continually perform a place, to bring its new forms into being: "new" compared to the fixed forms at stake when place is considered reducible to being a unit or part of space, a passive segment of a volume that is regarded as itself metrically definite—up to the limit of infinite space. With plants, we are talking of something that is not only located in a place but is itself place-generative.

While the beginning of growth is ofttimes aleatory, there is nothing haphazard about its ongoing patterns. Having received various types of information about the surroundings, a seedling *places* new leaves and shoots in the most adventitious spots.[3] The investment of energy that goes into this endeavor is so high that it can be a matter of life and death; especially in environments with little resources, the plant's decision on the exact site of new growth, further extending roots and shoots, the decision that arises at the intersection of over fifteen environmental stimuli in plant signal processing, does not leave much margin for error. From a phenomenological vantage point, we might say that the deliberate *placement* of new organs allows the plant to forge (construct and construe) the place of its growth, meaningful (and, hence, livable) from its unique standpoint and physical position. It follows that, while entailing receptivity, a place (not least the place of plants) is a cumulative outcome of enactments by those whose place it is outside the confines of active appropriation or passive inclusion in it. In other words, plant life teaches us that places are dynamic intersections of implacement and self-placement.

The insight emerging here is profound: the sessility of plants, rather than being a factor of a sheerly passive being, not only tolerates radical mutation but itself consists in such mutation. And this mutation is not merely external—a matter of the exact shape of plants, which varies greatly from species to species as well as within the plants of a given species: indeed, from one plant to the next—but of their ways of being-on-and-in-earth, both by themselves and in relation to other plants as well as to multiple forms of life, including, but not restricted to, human life.

The place of plants may be stationary and preclude locomotion compared to that of inherently mobile animals, including that of humans. But there can be no doubt that it is a very active life that deserves its own description and discussion at the limits of *phytophenomenology*. This is what we offer in this short book, which aims to do justice to the placiality of plants as well as to a broader understanding of places beyond the presuppositions of motility—hence, of the possibility of displacement—that tend to provide us with unconscious filters, or taken-for-granted practical axioms, as far as a phenomenology of place is concerned.

II

Note that our preliminary discussion of plants so far has been saturated with humanoid claims and modes of description. Yet, the larger task is to try to understand plants as much in *their* terms as in ours alone. What would this shift in emphasis entail? We cannot give up recourse to human language and thus to our own characteristic forms of thinking; after all, you are now reading a text composed of words that present arguments and insights that are undeniably human in their formulation even if they aim at describing decidedly nonhuman ways of life. But we as authors can attempt to push the limits of language farther out than is usually attempted in most prose descriptions. One of us (MM) has dubbed such an effort "meeting the plants halfway."[4] This we shall start to do by attending to several paradoxes—the first two being closely related to each other and the third essential to this book as a whole.

Paradox # 1: when plants are fully stationary, they are likely to be alive and well. When humans are immobile, they are sleeping, seriously ill, or dead. The medical phrase "vegetative state" expresses this paradox well.

Paradox # 2: while plants are sessile without special effort—this is their mode of being-in-the-world—humans often have to undertake strenuous efforts to become fully recumbent: not only do they have to slow down but to *settle down*, and this is sometimes far from easy if they are agitated or if the world is very demanding or otherwise lacks quietude at the time. Deep meditative practices that take years of painstaking training are required in order to achieve such a condition.

Paradox # 3: yet both these very different modes of being take place *in place*. Place somehow subtends each situation—both inherent sessility and equally inherent mobility. How can this be? What is it about place that underlies each of these opposed modes of being despite their stark divergences? Answering this is essential to the basic project of this book overall. At this early point, we shall consider only one way to resolve the first two paradoxes, leaving the third paradox to be addressed in section 4.

III

It is not sufficient to say, as we just did, that place "subtends" or "underlies" plant stationariness and human mobility.[5] More is involved, more is at stake than being under-lying—which is a mere descriptor for the empirical fact that we humans tend to deem place, at a first level of consideration, what is underfoot when we are standing or walking. Indeed, here plants are themselves akin to places, even etymologically so. As Walter Skeat notes in the entry for "plant": "1.—Lat. *planta*, a plant; properly, a spreading sucker or shoot. From the base PLAT, spreading, seen in Gk. *platus*, spreading, broad.—PLAT, to spread out; see Place. The Lat. *planta* also means the flat sole of the foot; hence, 'to plant one's foot,' i.e., to set it flat and firmly down."[6] *Plant* is, therefore, a basically agricultural term for vegetal being: it refers to those varieties of such being that can be grown and cultivated there where the soil has been flattened and rendered appropriate to field crops—and, by extension, on any stretch of earth that supports plants of a given kind. Subtly domesticated by being semantically uprooted from forests or mountainous ecosystems, where geology and ecology are precisely not flat, "plant" is also determinate with regard to its place.

That said, places (and plants) are of still greater scope and significance than this:

1. For one thing, place is not always *under* bodies, animated or not. It is as much *around* sensitive beings as beneath them—where "around" may include a dimension of under but much more as well: namely, its being *outspread*, the way it extends outward and beyond the very locus of a given organism as well as beneath it. And such aroundness may even include a factor of

being *over*—as when a plain on which we are now situated arcs abruptly upward so as to become a mountain: as with the flatlands of western Kansas and eastern Colorado as they turn abruptly into the Rocky Mountains that emerge dramatically from these lowlands. Here our look goes *upward* as we take in the mountains before us. The active role of the head is telling, and all the more so in that its metaphysical import in the Western tradition aligns two vertical systems of meaning, the corporeal and the axiological. So, the highest point of the body in the upright bipedal posture matches the highest mental capacity (ratiocination) that is regarded as at once uniquely humanizing and closest to the divine or eidetic realms. With plants and places, harking back to the Latin *planta*, it is usually the other way around: majestic as they may be, both are subjected, physically and metaphysically, to the lowest position imaginable, literally underfoot, despite their being outspread and despite their possibility of being over us. Even as I gaze up at the Rocky Mountains, I am aware that I am doing so from a flat plain to which my feet (and my car if I am driving) are confined.

2. But being under, around, or over offers only the first of three ways in which place is a primary presence for plants and human animals: namely, by its *directionality*. Equally important is the way in which place offers a meaningful *scene-of-presentation* for all that moves on it or grows in it. "Place" names this scene— "scene" being a word that in its original Greek form of *skené* signifies booth, tent, and (more generally) stage. (*Nota bene:* this stage itself, like all others, allows for an interplay of light and shadows, of the hidden in the wings or backstage and the revealed, an open flat and hard surface propping up the action— *that upon which* whatever or whoever appears makes an appearance—and the depth allowing for exits and entrances,

perspective and movement.) The place of plants, as well as of humans and much else, is a *presentational scene* where the phenomenal presence of something can appear—whether that thing be a mite, a mouse, or a mountain. *Place* as we are using the term makes all this possible as a basis for what is presented there: sent forth for the apprehension of whoever or whatever is able to take it in. Place in this second acceptation is thus a *scene of display*—where things and events, people and plants and animals, hills and mountains, show up and present themselves to be seen, grappled with, noted, manipulated, admired, or reviled, including from a plethora of perspectives of other-than-human beings. It is the basis of the "there" that comes forward from whatever "here" belongs to percipient beings of many kinds.

3. Place is also *dynamizing*. It is not just a resting place but a place where things happen, as in a scene or on stage, sometimes routinely and sometimes in novel ways that cannot be anticipated (though, eventually, most of them can be understood, scientifically or otherwise). It is more than the mere locus or occasion of such happenings even if it may be very tempting to reduce it to this for the sake of convenience. Instead, it often actively contributes to the happening of the event by providing the force and the inspiration for this event: a *taking place* without either seizing or appropriating it in anything like an exclusive manner. For many things would not happen at all but for the place they are in and from which they take their inspiration. For example, certain crops cannot thrive except in certain soils. This is not just a matter of an efficient-causal nexus but of the *active possibilizing* that certain soils (and in viniculture the ensemble of what is called *terroir*) enable and others do not. Far from being a merely sodden presence, the right kind of soil engages the seeds of certain plants to flourish in their presence—to come into their own,

sometimes in new and unexpected ways (as with the creation of new species or new variants of given species, not to mention the mutations triggered by soils that are laced with radionuclides as in the vicinity of Chernobyl or Fukushima) that break with existing patterns.

4. Place is *sustaining*. Again, like a stage, it provides support from below and all around. But it is also sustaining in the sense of nourishing, rather than merely propping up. In the case of plants the two senses of sustaining—physically supporting and nourishing—are interlaced in the stabilizing and osmotically operative presence of the root system of a plant. The roots convey water and other nutrients to the upper parts of plants. Soil itself is sustaining; this helps to explain its importance in raising crops. A depleted, acidified, or salinized soil cannot sustain whatever may be planted on it. Soil supports life, especially plant life that must count on its combination of resiliency and firmness. In effect, all the classical elements (earth, air, fire, and water) are sustaining for plants, even if they are not all underlying: it was not by chance that, in one of their first formulations in Ancient Greece, Empedocles referred to the elements as *riza*, "roots." But domestic places are sustaining as well, especially when they contain features that suggest memories important to residents—memories that sustain their sense of continuity and well-being. The destruction of such placial supports undercuts a sense of an open and auspicious future. Place here shows dimensions that cannot be reduced to objectively spatial parameters and actively involve temporality or time-consciousness.

5. Finally, place is *consolidating:* it brings together the four traits we have just singled out by generating ever new and unexpected combinations. Such consolidation helps to explain why finding the right home-place is so highly valorized in virtually

every human society.[7] For it is in a home-place that a dynamized scene-of-presentation occurs in a quite routine way, as this is made accessible in rooms that provide space for mutual support. Plants have their own equivalents of such consolidation, though these are largely underground among the tangle of roots that, regarded as a single mass, are the equivalent of a home-place that acts as a sustaining presence in and through the life of a given plant. In broader terms, the appropriateness of plants to particular climates (say, tropical plants that cannot survive well in northern latitudes) exemplifies such home-places, as does the general and particular neighborhood where they thrive, or not, depending on the other species of plants growing next to them, the availability of sunlight or sun exposure in the places of their growth, and similar factors. Seen under this lens, recent climate change may be regarded as a planetary-scale loss of home-places, a displacement of the places themselves, subsequently of the plants growing there, and then of masses of other environmental refugees.

IV

You may recall that the third paradox we've mentioned has to do with how very different modes of being take place *in place*. One way to approach this paradox is through two rather informal, colloquial and basic, references to places as *here* and *there*.

"Here" is the place where we are at this particular moment. Wherever we are, we are always *here*. Yet, for human beings, as for all mobile animals, the *here*, wherein we find ourselves, is transitory. For us, it can become something that is "over there" as soon as we abandon the spot where we sit or stand, and, consequently, it is converted into a "nowhere," without affecting us—who will survive its destruction—in the core of our being. The possibility of a *here* becoming a *there* defines both the sense and, when it is acted upon, the consequences of mobility. So, even if we are here right now, our minds are likely wandering elsewhere, and our bodies will follow suit soon. As we experience it, being-here throws us into the flux of time, with its short- and long-term plans and expectations of not-being-here-any-longer, but rather over-there, which, having momentarily been experienced as another *here*, will also be forsaken, becoming a *there* once again—albeit now in relation to a fresh *here*. This apparently very simple and banal observation forces us to put into perspective our relation to a place, which is, by the same token, a relation to the places between which we circulate.

That is also how Hegel's *Phenomenology of Spirit* begins, as it puts into relief the instability and self-negation of the *here*. In the ever-shifting world of "sense-certainty," every *this* supplanted by another singularity passes into *that*, every *now* becomes a *then*, and every *here*—an *over there*. Just listen to the German philosopher's formulation: "'Here' is, for example, the tree. If I turn 'round, this truth has vanished and is converted into its opposite: 'No tree is here, but a house instead.' 'Here' itself does not vanish; on the contrary, it abides constant in the vanishing of the house, the tree, etc., and is indifferently house or tree."[8]

As a rejoinder to Hegel, whose example of a tree replaced with a house right *here*—in the paradigmatic "here" of phenomenology—is very suggestive in the era of global deforestation, we may ask: what if a tree were not just something *here*, objectively placed before us, but *another sort of place*, the center-point of its own world with a distinct orientation toward its environments? In that case, the obliteration of its milieu would signify the end of a plant's world and of its life, for, unless it were transplanted by a human being, it would perish along with its *here*. A plant's sense of place, mediated by sensitivity to multiple environmental factors and their interactions, is distinct from that of the human. Before and beneath the heady phenomenology of spirit lies an uncanny phenomenology of the vegetal. It is the confluence of human and plant phenomenologies of place around the *here* and the *there* that we shall navigate to the best of our abilities.

The phenomenological sense of sessility implies a relation to place as the *here*, devoid of the possibility of relocating *over there*. Rather than being a limitation, or a set of negative traits, the place of plants evinces the *absolutizing of the here*, a nondialectical practice of being-here that does not allow this particular *here* to vanish without essentially affecting the living being who is here. Human experience in late modernity follows the opposite trajectory of *absolutizing the there*, such that every *here* is experienced as already *over there* before we have even moved out of the place where we are at this very moment.[9] That is: the sense of place, as experienced by human beings, is caught up within a complex historico-ideologico-technological framework of displacement, which accentuates and exaggerates the definitional characteristics of nonsessile beings and which makes these latter paradigmatic for all beings.

There is nothing more difficult for us at this moment in history than to linger patiently in the *here* without as much as fantasizing about something that lies over there, where we are not. Such a difficulty is biologically as well as historically contingent, with respect to the range, frequency, technical capacities, and desirability of displaceability. Martin Heidegger, for his part, understood human existence precisely as the possibility of "being-there" (not here, despite the literal translation of existence, or

Da-sein). By implication, he deemed other living beings, tethered to the immanence of the *here* and to the pure present, to be outside the sphere of human existence. The plant's complex relation to the places of its growth and outgrowth testifies to the problematic nature of this assumption.

We aim to broach the theme of how different modes of being (say, vegetal and human) take place in place. Perhaps, this is because different modes of place take place in place: preeminently, the *here* and the *there*, along with their respective absolutizations. And a place as such, in its very placiality, is only viable *either* in and as this dynamic, partial, and constantly adumbrated convergence of the *here* and the *there or* as the sessile exploration of an absolute *here*. Hegel prefers to explain it dialectically, when he notes that the "'here' itself does not vanish; on the contrary, it abides constant in the vanishing of the house, the tree, etc." Regardless of our displacement, moving without pause *over there*, we will always find ourselves right here, in the *here* that the previous *there* has become for us, if only momentarily. The *here* still lays its claim on the absolute. Thus, the sense of place in phenomenology (including Hegel's) is implicitly yet insistently vegetal, underneath all the accelerating displacements and absolutizations of the *there*.

But, *pace* Hegel, the inherent negation of the *here* that makes it what it is does not translate into the abstract and formal indifference of a place as a *placeholder* for whatever and for whomever. Whether sessile or mobile, for the one who is here the rich and ultimately inexhaustible details of the *here* matter, even if, for sessile existence, they matter more because the very fate and life of a stationary organism are tied to this *here*. Last but not least, there are various *here*s in every *here*—mine and that of a tree, of the bee and the squirrel who visit it at the same time as I do, of the fungi and microbes attaching to its roots, and so on. The multitude of places gathered in place elucidates, and to some extent resolves, our third paradox.

V

Clearly, place is multidimensional. This very feature helps to explain at once its pervasiveness—it is everywhere in plant and animal worlds: their worlds are *place-worlds*—as well as its importance for any adequate assessment of life on earth. It is a dimension of dimensions, an element of elements. And yet, it has been systematically overlooked or, if recognized, misunderstood as a mere modality of space, subject to quantification and striation. *Striation* is Deluze and Guattari's term for space that is quantifiable: as in modern mapping. To striated space they oppose *smooth space*, which is none other than *place* as we have been describing it. This is exemplified by their understanding of *nomad space*, which is the trajectory of nomadic movements between various preestablished locations—the equivalent of a series of places between which a given nomadic group moves on a periodic basis, with variations induced by weather and certain practical considerations. Thus is established, and continually reanimated, a *placial circuit*. Such a circuit, even if nonpermanent, sustains and consolidates a given nomadic group's collective life.[10]

We know that the migration of certain animals follows a pattern not unlike that of human nomads: bison, elk, and still other species. When such patterns are interrupted—as has happened at the U.S.-Mexico border wall (*La Frontera*)—it can be disastrous to the survival of the members of the species in question. Less familiar is the surprising fact that something very much like this holds true for certain plants that exhibit their own nomadism. In seeds, spores, and pollen, plants condense themselves, distilling their being into something portable. (A tumbleweed diaspore deviates from this rule, as virtually the entire plant detaches from the root to roam the earth in the wind.) By and large, they travel light, packing the bare minimum indispensable for future growth elsewhere, the growth destined to be shaped by and eventually to shape the seed's landing site that, as the seed germinates, *will metamorphose into the place of the mature plant.*

How plants are dispersed is significant in its own right. Letting the diaspore and its contents drop down to earth or entrusting it to the wind, the pollen attaching to butterfly wings, or the seeds wending their way to another place in the stomachs of birds—all these acts are awash with the contingencies of carrying and of landing. In throwing themselves, in opening themselves up to dis- or relocation, plants throw their fates to chance. As a compensation for the uncertainty of the outcome, they increase the number of throws, following a near infinity of possible trajectories, some of them bound to succeed even if a vast majority fails. This may be said to point toward a notion of *the event of plants,* both dovetailing with and diverging from the processes of human migration and diasporic dispersion.

The placiality of plants is a virtual *terra incognita,* and we are here providing a first concerted consideration of what such placiality consists in. Increasingly more will be discovered on many fronts as the life of plants is further explored by botanists and plant scientists. But place as such is unlikely to figure in these investigations, given that it resists strict scientific determination. And it does so because it is mainly an experiential matter whose proper understanding is phenomenological, not scientific. Our own approach in this book is largely, if sometimes loosely, phenomenological. We take up how we ourselves experience plants as well as how plants themselves can be said to experience their worlds, whether these worlds are contiguous with our own human worlds or not, while also indicating the points of contact or occasional intersections between these two experiences.

2

PERIPHERAL POWER

Structural Dynamics at the Edges of Plants

Here we take up a special aspect of the material ontology of plant and tree life: the various ways that certain dynamic structures inherent in such life contribute to what is unique in that life: edges, borders/boundaries, and modes of mobility and kinesis. Each of these structures contributes substantially to the deconstruction of the common idea that plants are passive beings, clinging to the ground as if too weak to do anything else: barely budging, as if stuck in place. Individious comparisons, tacit or explicit, are made between the often-dramatic movements of animals, human and otherwise, as in improvised dancing or other forms of active bodily behavior. A plant dancing? This seems an impossibility, an outright contradiction in terms.[1] And yet we have already seen ways in which plants are mobile and not altogether sessile. Our attention was for the most part drawn to the internal dynamics of plants: their metabolism, as it were. But we have not paid sufficient heed to ways that plants reach out and surpass themselves—how they live and thrive at their own edges, creating (and *being*) effective borderline presences in the natural world thanks to their own unique intentionalities.

I

The edges of plants are not merely where plants end—where they give out. Only from one perspective is this the case: the failure to occupy more space, a dropping-off of vegetal substance. But this is a very limited perspective that relies on such dubious modernist assumptions as that empty space is passively there to be occupied by solid bodies with no significant interim states between these two exclusive extremes. Hybrid states on this view are held to be nonexistent, reflective of cognitive confusion on the part of anyone who posits such states. This is not to deny that the edges of material things do *drop off*—that is, disappear from clear sight. But the drop-off itself is often gradual and can be complicated by various intermediaries: as when the arm of the chair on which I am now writing doesn't simply vanish but gives way to various supports under the arm. *Visually*, the arm's edge as viewed from above may seem to give way to nothing else; but I can *feel*, with my hand, the underneath of the chair arm; or I can *sense* that there is something else there after a lifetime of sitting in comparable chairs. Such feeling and sensing rely upon body memory, which intervenes to supply what is manifestly missing from direct visual perception.

More generally, ocularcentrism misleads us when it comes to the edge-world, including that which pertains to the places of plants. It attempts to operate between the exclusive poles of Being and Nothingness: being-in-sight and being out-of-sight, what is visible and what is invisible. Touch is a better guide: I can reach down and tell right away what lies under the upper arm of the chair in which I am sitting. After a long history of sitting in chairs, I am confident that I will find some kind of supporting structure there.

Vision is an inadequate—even a misleading—guide to the ongoing perception of my lived world. It is all the more deficient when it comes to the lived world of plants. Looking at a bush sporting bright orange tendrils that is before me just now, I cannot tell just how this plant is configured in the parts that I cannot see clearly, nor can I directly visualize its vast subterranean portions, the root system with its symbiotic cross-species assemblages. It is not that I suspect the edges of its branches, leaves, and tendrils that I can now perceive will give way to something entirely different, much less to sheer nothingness. Rather, I am reasonably confident that the view from the other side of this plant will be continuous with what I take in from the side presented before me. Viewed from the other side, I know I am likely to encounter something very much like the same gay orange blossoms and light green leaves and branches that I now perceive, even if differently configured. Surprises will be small as I circulate about a plant that I am confident is *one coherent living being*.

A considerable part of my confidence in the continuity of succeeding presentations of this bush is due to its being anchored in place: to its being *one plant in one place*. This place is its own place, the place of this one living thing, comprised of a multiplicity of growths. Especially notable here is that this place has *no determinate edge*. It is *where* the plant is, yet it is not itself visible, much less measurable or discrete. We struggle to find the right language to name it. Terms that come to mind are "base," "area," "spot" but these are notably indeterminate. If the edges of parts of the plant here in place are finite and describable— such that I can say that a given tendril is approximately two inches in length—the edges of the place where the plant presents itself are neither visible nor measurable nor fixed once and for all. They escape exact determination, even an approximate one such as I can give for its tendrils, branches, and roots.

We soon begin to suspect something remarkable is happening here—remarkable from the standpoint of any world in which determinate measurement prevails. We are in a realm in which any such measurement is absent and does not obtain; it is unavailable and even inappropriate. But, certainly, the place of a plant does exist as the place of the plant that it underlies. It is a positive presence even if one whose edges are not only not measurable but indeterminate by any set standard. And yet it *is* the place of the plant before me as I write these lines. This I cannot doubt. But then what *is* it? More generally, what is the place of plants? Where is it? These are primary questions we seek to address in this book—questions about something intrinsically indeterminate, starting with the edges of the extent of a place as it underlies and supports a given plant.

We are here pointing to a remarkable feature of plant life: their places are inherent and real yet do not possess the kind of edges that characterize the sort of places we associate with lawns and lots that are defined by their outer edges—edges at once visible and measurable. Such radical indeterminacy does not mean that the places of plants lack edges altogether; rather, we are encouraged to conceive of a special sense of edge characteristic of such places. Since every place has some kind of edge, however minimal—otherwise, it would be endless altogether—we are left to wonder what kind of edge is here at stake.

It is fair to say that we are dealing here with an edge that is inherently *amorphous*. The place of a plant may seem edgeless at first consideration; but this is only because we presume all edges to be determinate in extent, relatively stable and nearly unchangeable. It is true that most edges of most things we encounter do have edges that invite measurement, or at least fairly definite verbal description, including the edges of *parts of* plants as with the tendril of the bush blossoming before me. But the edges of places—starting with the places of plants—are something else.

A first paradox is that such places are edgeful in their very indeterminacy. Think of encountering a row of trees that grow spontaneously as a cluster in a given field and that have *their own place*—a place whose outer edge is so amorphous that we cannot say just where it begins or ends. Yet we cannot deny that it *is* a place; indeed it is *their place*. The same holds true for any plant or tree or groupings of these same beings. If they have places in the world of the living, they have edges, even if these edges cannot be seen or touched or made determinate otherwise. For every place carries with it its own edges, inaccessible as these may be by any customary means of determination. Just as every plant or tree has its own place, every place has its own edge, however elusive this edge may be.

So we reach here the apex of the paradox: the places of plants are at once real—based in soil, part of a larger realm of "land"—yet their edges resist any exact specification. Such edges are not only inexact—implying the possibility of more precise measurement—but radically *anexact*.[2] The kind of edges they have is experientially indeterminate and will always be so.[3]

II

The edges of parts of plants themselves are quite different. In their case, we can see or feel quite directly that they begin and end at quite determinate loci: in the case of the bright orange tendril we spoke of earlier we can say quite unambiguously that *here* is where it begins, and *there* it ends. It must be added that only *now*, at this very moment, is it the case that *here* is where the tendril begins and this *there* is where it ends. The ongoing growth, decay, and metamorphosis of plants render their edges changeable, mobile, and temporally indeterminate. The changeability of edges holds for all material existence over greater or lesser stretches of time, but it is especially pronounced in the world of plants, which are practically defined by these changes. For, where a given vegetal edge dropped off both visually and substantially just a week ago, this edge may be extended further thanks to the buds appearing on the magnolia tree I have been contemplating, or it may drop off well before the point at which it did so due to the shedding of foliage in the fall. Vegetal edges are thus *self-adumbrating* in their attunement to their organic and inorganic others: the perspectives onto the world embodied in plant structures are mutable, depending on the seasons, environmental conditions, availability of moisture and other nutrients, the points at which a plant is in its reproductive or growth cycles, and so forth.

And the same is true of the branches of the plant on which the tendril is located. The edges of both are hybrid in the sense we specified earlier whereby their yet unseen sides unfold in certain largely expectable ways as we move around them, just as the potential organs that are dormant in the meristems may grow and unfold in somewhat *un*expectable ways in tune with the seasonally changing dynamics of the place. Meanwhile, there is never any doubt that they *do have edges*—and that these can be described verbally or photographed. The branches and tendrils are at least that determinate at the precise moment in time when we approach them. By the same token, their own particular places, which are far from haphazard, determined as they are by the plant's decision regarding their placement and regarded as loci on the plant of which they are an integral part, are determinable at least verbally and often even mathematically (as being so many centimeters in height or length). The amorphousness of placement that obtains for the plant as a whole does not hold for its particular parts (branches, leaves, roots): here place collapses quickly into site—precisely what is not the case for the place of the whole plant of which they are organic parts.

We are here faced with the paradoxical situation whereby plants are at once precisely edged and placed (with regard to their particular growing, decaying, metamorphosing or, in a word, mutable parts) and yet are amorphous when it comes to the place and edge of the plant as a whole. Strange ambiguity, strange situation.[4]

We are reminded of the dense dialectic between *here* and *there* discussed earlier. Just as there is no fixed Here that can be placed in direct contraposition to There—one always evolving into the other in (indeed, *as*) lived experience—so the edge of the place of a plant entails a dense dialectic between precision and imprecision: precision not as measurable but as being the edge of the place of *this* particular plant and this plant only (or, ampliatively, of this coherent group of plants), imprecision as an edge that is not measurable in inches or feet or any other exact metric, which must be there (for every place has to end somewhere, thus has to have an edge), but *just where* is not easily, if ever, determinable. It follows that, via what presents itself as the imprecision of the edges of their places, plants both occupy and persistently change their *placial* positions. In this way, they respond and better correspond to the temporally variable textures of their milieu, which they also cocreate. The imprecision of the places of plants is indicative of the ongoing activities of sense-making by the plants themselves. Spatial expressions of vegetal intentionality, the ever-shifting edges of plants are, in a quite nonmetaphorical vein, their gestures, amounting to their expression and body language.

III

If we are not to be stymied by this aporia of precision/imprecision, we need to rethink edge itself. An edge, rather than being the outer limit of something—"the limit of a solid" as Socrates put it at *Meno* 76a, that is, where it *stops dead*—can exceed itself. It can be strictly speaking *ecstatic*, exceeding its current limits. The self-exceeding of edges in plants constitutes their growth, and so it is not confined to plants that are hyperdramatic in their displays: say, a bird-of-paradise. It can be found in the bare stem of an ordinary plant or the leaf mass of a nearby tree. Let us take the example of the *branch* of the same plant with orange blossoms we have invoked previously (figure 2.1).

We say guilelessly that the limbs (of trees) or stems (of plants) *branch out*. This phrasing attempts to capture the dynamism of growth in both cases: the way that limbs and stems are not altogether static but press outward and onward as if by some inner *nisus*, which is, however, exceptionally attuned to everything that is going on outside the plant. (Henri Bergson's notion of *élan vital* attempts to capture the same force at a metaphysical level.) This dynamism is most vividly seen in the outer edges of what branches out and in the meristems, dotting an existing branch—especially its tips. It is as if these edges *lead the way* of outward and onward growth rather than merely containing or encapsulating it. They embody the forward thrust of branching *out*—a branching out that is often also characteristically a branching *up*. The dialectic of the out and the up amounts to a situation whereby a given plant exceeds itself: presses beyond its strictly material limits and in so doing puts into question the metaphysical categories of identity, including self-identity.

In so doing, the plant propels itself beyond what is also characteristic of it: namely, its *settling down*—down into the soil from which it springs and in which its roots also branch, unless they are bulbs or fibrous roots of about the same size. Such settling down embodies its sessility: its comparative immobility. With

Figure 2.1. Plant leaves reaching out. Photograph on-site by E. Casey, August, 12, 2022.

plants overall, we encounter edges that can send our look or touch up and out as well as down and into. The two implicit movements are complementary to each other and obey "the thing itself"—the polarization of plant growth extending up and down simultaneously. This is just what we might expect from a close analysis of the edges of living things such as plants. Rather than being static and terminal, their edges are characteristically two-way. They are perceived as tending out and up in a decisive forward thrust as well as descending down into an invisible rooted underground mass. The intentionality of plants is inherently double; it goes both ways at once.

The ancient image of the burning bush (*Euonymus alatus*, colloquially known as winged spindle) captures what we are here discussing. This is a bush that thrusts up from within its own resources—so intensely that it bursts into flame. We need not take this image literally to actively imagine that bushes have their own internal thrust, their own "operative intentionality" in Maurice Merleau-Ponty's phrase. This thrust is shown graphically in the outspreading of plants; as when we perceive their branches, leaves, and blossoms as reaching out and up from earlier origins in the roots and trunk or stem of the plant to which they belong. This thrusting is intensified in the case of the burning bush, which presents itself as engaging in an *ec*-static movement: as going *out* from the stasis of immobility. It is as if such ecstasis were compensating for the otherwise salient sessility of plants. But the same burning bush is also undeniably rooted in the soil beneath it: it comes from somewhere *under* the inflamed crown of the bush.

More generally, any liveliness or vitality we are tempted to ascribe to plants is an intentionality made most manifest in the perceived or implied directionality of its manifest edges.

This directionality is two-way. It may not be perfectly balanced in our perception of it—the edges of a burning bush are more manifestly upward than downward in their perceived thrust—but there are always traces of both directions as we encounter such a plant and its many less dramatic fellow members of the plant kingdom. Thriving in two worlds at the same time—the subterranean and the aerial—plants also appropriately direct themselves to the resources each offers: water and minerals below ground, solar energy above. The physiology of their growth as well their ec-static edges are congruent with their dual intentionality, according to which certain aspects of the plants' milieu *stand out* and *make sense* to the roots or to the shoots in a relation of *mutual fitting*. There is neither totalizing organismic integration nor compartmentalization and utter disintegration as a result. In a loose living alliance, the below- and the aboveground portions of the same plant pursue their own activities. In most cases, these do not have to be communicated to the rest of the plant, for instance, through biochemical or electrical signaling or calcium pathways. Only in extreme situations, such as a drought, does the need arise to share information and ensure a temporary *uniformization of vegetal intentionalities*, aligning their upper, lower, and lateral edges.

IV

From this analysis of the bidirectionality of the perceived and the perceiving, as well as the thinking, accomplished by the edges of plants, we can conclude that edges, rather than being the inert end points of surfaces, are genuine *events*. Not only do things happen at the edges of plants; they happen *as these edges themselves*. Far from being static as merely liminal, edges are themselves *eventmental*. They are where things occur and where various vectors of intentionalities intersect. Uniquely so: there and nowhere else in such a decisive way. They not only occasion things; they are themselves occasions: a version of what Nicolas Malebranche called "occasional causes."

As an example of the eventmental character of plant edges, let us consider the case of gardens, which can be considered to provide *stabilitas loci* for what is planted there. When we find ourselves in a garden that has predelineated paths, we find ourselves drawn by the edges that define these paths. These edges do not merely define the course of our walking if we take up their invitation; they call out to us to follow their lead: "come our way," they seem to say, adding that "you will find this way rewarding." Of course, they are not speaking to us in so many words—or words of any sort—but they are felt to *issue an invitation*: to be welcoming us to the garden world whose effective edges they constitute. Their configuration is not only prescribed according to the plan of the landscape architect—say, André Le Nôtre at the Gardens of Versailles or the anonymous planner of a modest city garden—and it is not reducible to geometric form even if it is regarded (as in the case of Versailles) as a "formal garden." Something else is going on here. The visitor is drawn into a drama of edges—an entire edge-world. Some of the edges of the inhabitants of this world are carefully shaped as trimmed to the point of their being almost linear, but other edges allow a certain freedom of growth, as if to remind the visitor that the bushes in the garden have a life of their own and configure themselves in their own characteristic way. The "figure" in *configure* is determined by edges, rough as well as regular. If the garden at

Versailles is viewed from above, we get this kind of pattern—wholly linear:

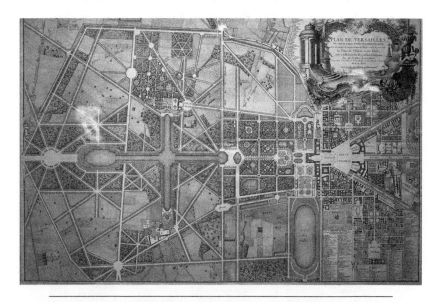

Figure 2.2. André Le Nôtre, full plan of Versailles, 1693.

But the same garden presents itself quite differently for the person who visits it in person. There, the paths, though fully directional and conventionally "straight," are edged by plants and small trees whose own edges are not altogether regular but manifest the kind of minor irregularities that the vast majority of all plants exhibit and that no formal or formalizing gardening practice can fully regularize or render homogeneous. As a result, to walk down the aisles at Versailles is to enter a sea of vibrant edges. This vibrancy is perfectly consonant with the formal regularity of the design of the garden as is evident in the image just shown. The result is a commixture of regular with irregular edges that do not distract but allure. The visitor walks the aisles of Versailles with assurance and confidence that she is being guided with a sure hand—the hand not only of Le Nôtre but of the bushes and trees that now populate the garden he designed more than 350 years ago (figure 2.2).

When there is no formal plan for a garden—as in the British gardens that emerged in the wake of Le Nôtre—but a situation in which the trees and other plants are allowed to take the lead, we observe a dialectic between the vegetative and the constructed, as at Stowe Gardens, designed by Charles Bridgeman, William Kent, and Capability Brown (figure 2.3):

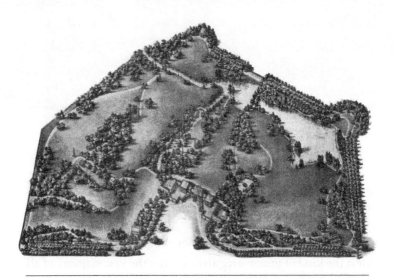

Figure 2.3. Stowe, as remodeled by Capability Brown.

Manifest here is the "wavy line," as it was called in the eighteenth century. It is still a *line*, but its very irregularity is mimetic of the way that naturally wooded areas create undulating patterns. Their contours are inviting to human visitors who have the sense that they are entering into a natural reserve and are welcome there. It is a congenial *place* in which they feel hospitably received by the natural world—at home there even if there are no houses or built structures to be encountered.

Alexander Pope said famously that humans "should consult the *Genius* of the *Place* in all."[5] The relationship between place and edge is very close. The two kinds of gardens just discussed are at once unique places of plants and other organisms inhabiting them, places for human ambulation and appreciation, as well as consisting in a congeries of artificial and naturally proffered edges. It is clear that there would be no place without edge: every place comes edged, however differentially and whatever its degree of formal indeterminacy—an indeterminacy that can be quite extreme, as we have seen in the case of the place of a single plant. Such a place is edged yet cannot be measured as such, indicating that not all edges are determinate if this means delineatable—traceable with a continuous line. But edges considered as events do not require delineation or measurement. They are *happenings* rather than physical entities, and as such they do not lend themselves to precise demarcation.

In the realm of edges, what matters most is *the power of the peripheral*. This is what edges exhibit when they are active and dynamic presences and this is the potentiality that is crucial to plants, proliferating largely on the peripheries of their emplacement. The exact form of this presence can vary greatly—from the rectilinear rows of the formal garden at Versailles to the curvaceous outlines and inlines of whole forests regarded as informal gardens as well as the pointed tip of a root that Darwin identified as where intelligence is located in the underworld of plants.[6] An edge need not be dramatic or demanding to possess peripheral power. Sometimes a quite tenuous edge can be of decisive significance—as with a bare branch of a plant that offers a perch for a blue jay who comes to alight on it. Nor need edges be humanly created or manipulated to possess potency: think of the way that the trees that encircle one in driving through a country landscape constitute a powerful presence, framing one's quite casual look even if they were not planted or tended by humans. Proof of such peripheral power is experienced even when easily discernible edges are almost altogether absent, as when driving across a desert. (In this latter case, the presence of a single barrel cactus can take on a virtually numinous force as a "sign of life.")

Plants are constituted by differential congeries of edges—whether those of the roots, the branches, or the bare leaves. This is not to discount the importance of the main bodies of plants. The perception of these bodies—their size, perceived force, etc.—certainly matters. But they too are edged in keeping with what emerges as a general rule in the experience of plants: *edges matter.* Edges make a difference, and sometimes the whole difference, between one plant and another, whether of the same or a different species, just as with animals and, indeed, virtually anything that inhabits the natural world, including bare rocks and stones.

The indispensable presence of edges extends to the place of plants. The fact that such a place can be so difficult to discern with precision is compatible with its being edged—edged in its own indeterminate way—and therefore living, mutable, and making sense (as well as a cumulative outcome of sense-making activities) not only for us but also, and in the first instance, to the plant whose place it is. If the place of plants is an event, it is a primary productive force in the life of plants. And this force not only has an edge, *it is itself an edge.* For place—not only of plants but of a myriad other things—is eventmental, and it is such thanks very much to its edges, determinate or otherwise.

For it is by its edges that a place becomes an *e*-vent: a "coming out" into the lived world of natural existence and growth. (And of decay as well: signs of disease and degeneration also show up in the edges of plants—in their withering and in other forms of contraction.) The life and times of plants are especially apparent in the surfaces of their branches, leaves, and roots: surfaces that possess edges. It is by the edges of their various surfaces that plants manifest their current state of being as well as what they are in the process of becoming.

V

Concluding Note on Borders and Boundaries. Strictly speaking, these are forms of edge, but they take on a special significance in plant and animal worlds. Borders are artificially determined, almost always by human beings—who establish them to fence things in or out, even if frequently they retrace natural divisions on the terrain: a mountain range, a river, or other rugged lines in topography or geological morphology. Subject to borders is a range of living things, from migrants to wolves. Invasive species of plants are also subject to exclusion by way of borders. In their case, a physical wall is often not necessary; bordering effects can be achieved by open spaces, trails of herbicides, and other such means—all of which are notably artificial, qua created almost entirely by human beings, and usually ineffective because of the plants' potent strategies of self-dissemination. They share with other kinds of bordering a common project of *exclusion,* whether of other human beings and certain animals or particular plants.

Most all such efforts at bordering have precise dimensions that lend themselves to linear layouts—most conspicuously in the case of border walls such as that constructed along the U.S.-Mexico border (*La Frontera*) in keeping with the 1848 Treaty of Guadalupe Hidalgo between the U.S. and Mexico. Even when not sanctioned by governmental agreements, most borders possess a certain impassability that makes movement over them difficult if not impossible: This Far and No Farther! We tend to think of this exclusionary function as true of human constructions, but there are analogues in the animal and plant world: for example, the changed composition of the soil and drier climatic conditions on the southern bank of a river, such as the Tagus, where vegetation differs from that growing on the northern bank. In all such instances, edges are the most conspicuous parts of the exclusionary structures—in some cases, carrying the exclusionary role by themselves alone; a constructed wall can be considered nothing but an outsized edge set in the earth.

Boundaries are something else. They are inherently porous, and though serving to demarcate one place or region from another they offer opportunities of transition between one place and another, one region and the next. When one approaches a grove of trees that is set in the farmland of Alabama, for example, the outer edge is unambiguous: just *here,* where I enter these woods, is the boundary between the flatland on which corn and cotton are being grown and the group of trees that make up the grove. Although the trees constitute a coherent mass and are dense in their clustering, I can both see into them and enter them on foot. Their outer edge is a permeable boundary that does not act to exclude but to allow a lover of trees to enter into their midst. The same is true for whole groups of plants as they populate a given place, as with a field of poppies in bloom; I can feel their welcoming presence as proffering an open receptivity to my entry into their midst at their outer perimeter, their receptive boundary, also welcoming in different ways birds and animals.

Borders and boundaries are primary ways in which places are configured at (and as) their edges, and we deal with them far more often than we might think. Everywhere we go—on foot, by automobile, even in airplanes—we find ourselves in their presence as basic structures of our life-world. Either they stand in our way or invite our way forward into their midst. Their edges offer to us a basic dyadic choice between being excluded and being included. This choice is perhaps most conspicuous in the case of the contrast between the aforementioned border wall at *La Frontera* and the open areas that are not yet walled in.[7] Where the border wall is unambiguous in what it signals to those attempting to get to the U.S. coming from Mexico—DO NOT ENTER THE U.S.—the unwalled areas are ambiguous: there is no concrete marker such as a wall there, yet there is an invisible imaginary line implicit in the soil: a line that can be easily traversed on foot (unless the Border Patrol or local vigilantes intervene to prevent this). In this stark choice, we see the differences between a border and a boundary in sharp relief.[8] In other instances, the differences are less obvious, and there are cases where what is at first perceived as a prohibiting border turns out to be an inviting boundary. When two of the author's (EC's) step-grandchildren recently encountered a thicket at the edge of a pathway in the local zoo, instead of being repelled they were drawn to enter into the thicket, where they discovered an entire labyrinth of passages inside that they proceeded to explore for the next hour: they had discovered a haven of connected boundaries.

Regarded as two major classes of edges, borders and boundaries can be contrasted as presenting clearly drawn outlines in the case of borders—enabling their mappable status in official surveys and various formal accounts—in contrast with the indistinct contours obtaining with boundaries. Otherwise put, borders are determinate enough to be regarded as *exact edges* whereas boundaries display indeterminate and *inexact edges*. As discussed earlier, this is the difference between edges that permit precise determination by whatever metric is appropriate to the circumstance and edges that resist such determination—so much so that their very indetermination is intrinsic to their being the edges they are.[9] At the U.S.-Mexico border, this contrast plays out in the dramatic difference between the presence of a fully built wall and a gap in the wall that is filled with fully grown trees, as in the Sabal Palm Sanctuary: the physical wall offers an exact edge that, precisely as determinate, is unambiguously discouraging to immigrants attempting entry into the U.S., while the sanctuary is characterized by gentle contours whose very amorphousness invites such entry.[10] Here we see that the difference between exact and inexact edges is not merely academic but has significant consequences in real life.

This chapter has explored the fate of edges as they circumscribe everything from the places of plants and the plant's own diversely presented surfaces to the perimeters of whole groupings of trees set in open fields. Rather than being reducible to the bare terminals of a leaf, a tree trunk, or an underground root, edges have shown themselves to be active presences, which, measurable or not, carry a dynamism of their own that animates a plant in whole or in part. They exhibit what we have called "the power of the peripheral"—according to which just where one might expect a living thing to be at its weakest, at the very area where it ceases to possess continuing substance as a material body, it manifests a special force that propels it in various directions that exceed what sheer physical limits alone can provide. Such edges *take us elsewhere* and *help us to think otherwise:* somewhere other than what their stationary form and bulk would permit regarded as in-themselves. The determinate and indeterminate edges presented by plants dynamize sheer material bulk and its bare limits, converting these into active *events of becoming*. They are where plants grow, decay, and metamorphose. This is in keeping with the premise that edges are eventmental; they are not mere things, or parts of things, but happenings whereby living things and their parts exceed their sheerly literal parameters and become active and mutable presences on their own terms.

Boundaries, which constitute a leading species of edge, are scenes of becoming in comparison with the inert borders they complicate by their ambiguous presence: inviting living beings into their ambient embrace in contrast with the enforced directionality characterizing constructed borders. They take us into another dimension of the places of plants—one that is essentially open: one can almost always enter through a boundary in more ways than one, just as one can move through a forest by several paths, preestablished or not. The breathable, porous boundaries that our own skin and plant leaves embody do just that. For boundaries open up while borders close down. Traffic through a border is either one-way or no-way, whereas we can move through a boundary in many ways. This is something that Paul Cézanne knew well as he daily walked the forests around his home in Aix-en-Provence on diverse paths—from many of which he glimpsed Mont Sainte-Victoire: differently enough in each case to paint this same mountain in hundreds of complementary ways. For him, the dense forests through which he walked were open boundaries through which he attained ever-new visions of a single commanding mountain.[11]

Interlude 1
HOW PLANTS THINK

Plants not only perceive but also *think* at their edges. According to a famous, if little understood, fragment of Parmenides, "it is the same thing for thinking and for being."[1] Modified for vegetal life, the dictum states that it is the same thing for plant-thinking and for plant-being, or, in other words, that plants, in the materiality of their growth, decay, and metamorphosis, think themselves into being and that they are what is thought through these activities. In their case, *I think, therefore I am* becomes *We grow, decay, and metamorphose, therefore we are.*

This manner of putting it recalls the notion of "growth-thought" (*phutikē noesis*) in Plotinus, which is his translation (inspired by the already cited Parmenidian fragment) of Aristotle's principle of vegetal vitality into "logical" terms. "Lives are thoughts in a way," Plotinus notes, "but one is a growth-thought [*phutikē noesis*], one a sense-thought, and one a mind-thought. How, then, are they thoughts? Because they are rational principles [*logoi*]. And every life is a thought, but one is dimmer than another" (*Ennead* III.8.8, 10–20).

The very idea of plant-thinking is greatly indebted to Plotinus. Nonetheless, our formulations diverge from his in three respects. First, plant-thinking rejects principles, logical or otherwise; it eschews absolute starting points, from which all else may be deduced. Second, the life-thought of plants is neither the dimmest nor the brightest nor some sort of an averaging out of the two. Thinking-living differently above and below the ground, a plant unsettles fixed associations with dimness and brightness in the realm of thought. Its mind does not slumber in the dark of the soil, as its roots skillfully navigate the mazes of mineral resources, water deposits, the roots of other plants, and so forth.[2] Vegetal life and thought are realized in actual plant lives and thoughts; they are sometimes at odds with one another even when they pertain to one and the same plant. And third, the logic animating plant-thinking and plant-living is that of the middle, excluded from the purview of formal logical systems.

If the place of thinking is in the middle, then to think is to juggle the extremes, existing with and in their mutual contradiction, including the fecund paradoxes we have been tracking in these pages. A life-thought lived between opposites that to us appear irreconcilable is not, itself, extremist, but *radical*, in that it radicalizes the extremes it interrelates, by rooting them in the middle. Juggled, the extremes are not extrem*ist*; they mutate into fecund middle edges.[3] Properly understood, such a nontotalizing and nonstatic world-integration is what growth accomplishes.

What immediately follows from our hypothesis is that formal, non- or antivegetal logic does not think.[4] Formal logic operationalizes the world and divides it into manageable compartments. Its principle of noncontradiction, denying the simultaneous validity and truth of X and not-X, justifies cutthroat competition, a life-and-death struggle that suffocates life itself, rendered indistinguishable from death. It forecloses the placiality of place. Its extremism transmutes *rigor mortis* from a postscript to a prelude for existence, a firm and secure foundation on which movement, life, and thought must be thought.

In addition to the bidirectionality of vegetal intentionalities, radical and radically nonextremist plant-thinking is evident in the coincidence of firmness and pliability in a plant that requires the support of cellulose cell walls and the stability of the trunk or the stem to lift it up, as much as the suppleness of the leaf and the petal, not to mention the probing sensitivity of root tips. To rely on both these extremes at once is to enact a process that is at the heart of what thinking is: rootedness and movement, structure and process, being-in-place and displacement, an elucidation that draws on inexhaustible secrecy and abstruseness. In a word, thought is growth, and plants enact such growth.

We have just asserted, almost in the same breath, that "to think is to juggle the extremes" and that "thought is growth." How to reconcile these two statements? How to balance them *in thought*? But, then, isn't growth itself a precarious balancing act, always on edge, rather than the relentless expansion, the monotonously quantitative augmentation it has come to be in modernity? Sustainable growth does not crave "more and more" but, on the contrary, revolves around knowing when to stop expanding and for how long—say, in the reproductive phase that is inversely proportional to the energy a plant invests into vegetative growth, during which it sends out new shoots, branches, and leaves. Growth is not ongoing quantitative increase (of extensions, dimensions, value, knowledge . . .)—this is its mutilated and truncated version that has reached us thanks to the double interventions of capitalism and the general quantification of existence in modernity. Viable growth is both intensive and extensive, its activity turned inward and outward. It sustains itself, too, with the byproducts of its own decay.

Generally, plant-thinking negotiates the contradictory demands of growth and reproduction that, at the functional level, correspond to the need for balance in the qualities of vegetal rigidity and nimbleness. There must be a negotiation between the phases or temporalities of growth and reproduction and, within the process of growth, between what is received from and what is returned to the world, not to mention between *what* grows, *how*, *when*, and *where*—all subjects to careful decision-making by plants. Even the fast and desperate elongation of the stem, eager to grow out of the shade and toward the light, is an expression of thinking: a precarious juggling act it performs allows it to leave the danger zone, albeit exchanging the robustness of what grows for pale and feeble stalks and leaves.

The ultimate extremes thinking must navigate are the thinker's self and its other. As we have already noted, cognition is not the purely interior process philosophers have taken it to be at least since early modernity, a sort of intensive growth uncoupled from the extensive unfolding of capital or political imperialism. The gulf Descartes espied between extended and cognitive realities is a distinction between two modalities of growing, each opposed to and implying the other. As soon as we reject the privatized, essentially Cartesian image of thought, it becomes clear that thinking is a dialogue or a plurilogue with the world irreducible to a symbolically mediated discussion. The "structure" of thinking is a conversation (a being-with-against: a mediation of extremes that, when they faced each other in absolute silence, claimed the status of self-sufficient, autonomous beginnings, incompatible with each other) and hence a construction in flux, invalidating the traditional distinction between "structure" and "function," or "structure" and "dynamics."[5]

Plants think at the edges of their bodies: on the surface of leaves, across their meristems, or at the tips of the roots, around which "transition zones" emerge, home to fungi, bacteria, and other microorganisms. There they converse with the world. The biosemiotic exchanges conducted in transition zones enable the roots to pursue an intelligent course of growth toward the most fertile and water-rich patches of soil. But thinking is not exhausted by intelligent conduct: it is doubtful that an intelligence said to be artificial can really think. Should we render the two terms synonymous, we would circumscribe the middle to a means for instrumentally posited ends or, more exactly, to usability. Treated as identical to intelligence, thinking turns into a metapragmatic tool utilized in order to attain anything that might be of use to the intelligent being in question.

On the flip side of intelligence, thinking is saturated with vital relations. Thinking happens for nothing, gratuitously, expressing the excess of existence over itself. "For nothing" means here not for oneself but "for the others," with the others encountered at the threshold of the self, which is constitutively open to them. To think is to be in a transition zone, to exist ec-statically at one's multiple edges. The plants' conversations with fungi, bacteria, other plants, etc., in root transition zones are much more (or much less) than a collaborative search for resources: they flesh out the sense of existence as a coexistence, its relational unfurling in an articulation of multiplicities irrespective of the boundaries separating different biological kingdoms, species, and specimens. Edges are *where* these conversations happen, and they are, themselves, happenings, the events of existence.

Extremes are radical rather than extremist, so long as they are the interfaces of the inside and the outside, self and other. The middle is an edge; it is where and when thinking takes place. Assessed in terms of the firing of neuronal synapses, the possibility of thinking in organisms with a central nervous system foregrounds the in-between, the intervals, the clefts separating the neurons that conduct electrical or biochemical signals. The more synaptic branches and, by implication, clefts there are, the more vigorous is cognitive activity.

Vegetal growth, which provides a model for neuronal arborization, is not at all different from this intensification of thinking. When axillary branches and lateral roots emerge, a plethora of opportunities arise for a plant to inhabit the intermediate space between itself and its milieu, to think better across a wide array of edges. This inhabitation fashions the very place of plants, as opposed to the site of their growth. The interfaces, proliferating thanks to a modular reiteration of existing plant structures in a deceptively redundant process, are the spatial expressions of a cogitation that no longer tallies with the Cartesian distinction between the extended thing and the thinking thing. In plants, intention is immediately extension: growth.

The freedom and fluidity of the in-between are inconceivable without a mix of the determinacy and indeterminacy of edges and extremes. If structuration is unsurpassable, then Hannah Arendt's suggestion to think "without a banister" (*Denken ohne Geländer*) is unacceptable.[6] Thinking happens *on* the banisters that are, to be sure, somewhat peculiar: made not of dead wood, not of timber, but of living trees. As she recommends removing the protections that guarantee the thinker's *security* (a word prevalent in contemporary political discourse, in the name of which terrible violations of human and other-than-human rights and existences are justified), Arendt beseeches her readers to take the risk embedded in genuine thinking. Such a risk entails the reaffirmation of the very banisters she wishes to get rid of, albeit with the modifications schematically outlined here. Insofar as a plant juggles the competing demands of growth and reproduction, what is above and what is below, its self and the others, it lives and thinks (lives-thinks) dangerously, always on the brink. Thinking is a risk worth taking. The alternative is worse: the greatest risk is not taking risks. At the level of their "species-being," plants know this exceptionally well, which is why they have lived and thought both more extensively and more intensely than we humans have managed to do thus far.

3

TAKING TREES OVER THE EDGE

We tend to think of trees as quintessentially nonhuman—as radically other than we are—standing solitary and stalwart, leading a life of their own, existing in ways we can barely understand. Trees go their own way, we go another. Or so we imagine . . .

Places are something else. They present themselves as prototypically human, especially insofar as they are where we *reside:* they are *there where we are.* Many of them are made for us, and some are made by us—made to be occupied. And if certain places are not directly habitable, we adapt to them or else modify them to fit our needs and interests. In this respect, places are, or can become human—sometimes all too human.

In this chapter we concentrate specifically on the places of trees. We investigate their places within a nascent phenomenological framework suited to them and we look at human places as they are experienced in interaction with those of trees. Our guiding set of questions includes the following: how do trees construe, shape, and get shaped by the places where they grow? In what ways might trees qua sessile beings relate to and cognitively map their habitats? What are the positive implications of the impossibility of getting out of such places, the immanence of their "here" unopposed to a "not-here?"

Our intention is to *give place back to trees*: to examine what kind of places they create and occupy, regardless of whether these places fit human dimensions or not and irrespective of whether we fit (into) them. In short, we aim at doing at least preliminary justice to the *mysterium coniunctionis* of trees and places. We shall discover several major ways in which this conjunction occurs, one of which is found in the way that the edges of places and trees interlace with each other. And it is from such considerations that we shall find trees and human beings converging in unexpected ways. By uncovering certain tacit affinities, we shall come to regard trees as our quiet companions on earth—just as we, at our best, are theirs as well.[1]

I

It is one thing to think of place as metrically determinable—measurable in repetitive units. Such is a site, which is not only measurable in this determinate way but part of a stretch of space that is suitable for some particular activity: that is, quite literally, *useful*. Hence the common phrase: "site *for* . . ." Site is what happens when place is construed as a matter of *space* regarded as a homogeneous medium. What is qualitative about a given place—its accessibility, its changing coloration, its very history—is rendered indifferent or nugatory when the place is construed as a site. Site is the fate of place when it is taken up in certain pragmatic or scientific contexts. Even if in these contexts it is basic and elemental, it is secondary to place as lived—as inhabited, mobilized, animated.

The placedness of trees cannot be reduced to their site specificity. Only for certain determinate purposes, such as the estimation of open land with an eye to its commercial value, is it so construable. But our interest in this book lies in determining the active emplacement of plants—the way they occupy the air that surrounds them as well as how they grow out of, and into, the earth, dynamically interacting with the soil in which they are rooted. Rather than a fixed entity, the place of plants is of a piece with their vegetal co-inhabitants, which means that, above and below ground, such places grow, decay, and metamorphose along with the plants themselves. Indeed, the sense of what is above and below (gravitropism) from the perspective of a plant relies on physiological cellular-level mechanisms available already to a germinating seed. It is vital to the proper development of plant organs (more precisely, their way of becoming placed: placing as a living activity) as with the shoots stretching up and the roots extending down, all on the body of a plant.

The place of trees is, therefore, always *places*, at least two in one—a *topos ouranios* and a *topos geinos*, chthonic and atmospheric—and an exuberant, proliferating multiplicity between the two. In twentieth-century French thought, trees have been taken as the living figures of *verticality*, from Paul Claudel's suggestion that "in nature, the tree alone is vertical, along with man" to Deleuze and Guattari's contrasting juxtaposition of tree structures with rhizomes.[2] The alleged verticality of trees implies the verticality of their places. How can we think through the logic of verticality in the case of the arboreal biaxial or bipolar existence? And how can we valorize such verticality rather than holding it up to critique and derision, as happens in the introduction to *A Thousand Plateaus*?

One early indication is found in a famous Heraclitus fragment: "the way up and the way down are one and the same" (*hodos anō katō mia kai ōutē*; fragment 60). But, when it comes to trees, they are not altogether the same: the upward movement thrusts toward an open *region*—e.g., the sky—while the way down leads into the enclosed nether region of the earth, which, for another pre-Socratic, Xenophanes, strives toward infinity (*apeiron*) beneath the upper limit (*peiras anō*) we tread with our feet (fragment 12, cf. Arist. de Coelo ii. 13; 294a 21). A lived verticality is, therefore, never simple; its coordinates and trajectories embedded in and between elemental milieus do not follow the rules of formal logic or mathematics. There is here the paradox that while trees are for the most part well anchored, they *give way*, or, more precisely, they *give ways* and can be said to *gesture toward* whole areas of the natural world, areas that extend down and up and, in both cases, *out*. The multiple extensions out from the tree itself—the extensions that, in an important sense, *are* the tree itself—merge with those extending out from its local or specific place, the *place of* the tree, where it is located, where it is to be found, and where it locates *itself*.

Coming off from the relatively uncomplicated linear form of a vertical section of the trunk between the roots and the branches, the lateral dimension of vegetal growth recedes to perceptual and ideational backgrounds. Nonetheless, the places of trees (both their habitats, such as forests, and the places that the trees not only occupy but themselves dynamically *are*) do not by any means limit themselves to the vertical axis alone. Due to the modular pattern of plant growth, the branching character of arboreality provides an image of *branching places*, of the place itself as a vertical, horizontal, and lateral branching out, opening unto other places by way of fresh interaction with the elemental realm. (We return to these "directionalities" in the last part of this chapter.)

A phenomenology of trees includes all the various ways in which aerial and earthen vegetal placing occurs: directionally, as vertical or horizontal or something in between; in terms of mode of engagement: with the air surrounding them and with the earth beneath them, etc. In these two very basic ways and others, we can say that a given tree finds or makes its place. *Its place*: this cannot be reduced to its pinpointable position, nor can it be adequately construed in terms of what Deleuze and Guattari call "striated space," that is, the occupation of space regarded as a universal medium that can be unitized in certain determinate ways. The place of trees is closer to "smooth space" in the nomenclature of *A Thousand Plateaus*: space that is configured by the way in which movement or other interaction occurs. But smooth space is conceived by these thinkers largely in terms of nomadic dispersions of human beings, whereas our concern is with the *local* facticity of trees—where "local" signifies *placial*.

The key to understanding the locality of place is its uniqueness. Such placement is always unique, *unilocal*, just here rather than there, yet expansive within the single locus to which a given tree or plant is confined. It is *expansive* within the limits of growth of a given arboreal or plant organism, while offering a *place-within-a-set-of-places* whose outer limits are terrestrial and aerial *regions*. Nevertheless, it is the place of *just this tree, only that plant*. How this place compares with other places is a matter of comparative indifference: "comparative" because it is of concern mainly to the scientist, the grower, the owner—who characteristically think of tree-placement in terms of site, where the just-here is what it is mainly with regard to a larger tract of land or earth, that is, to *all that space*.

II

Our aim here is to understand the *singularity of tree placedness and placing*: what makes it unique in each and every case, just *this place* and not its position in a generic (much less universal) space. And yet such placement also has certain features that obtain for other trees as well, both as individuals and as members of the same species.

Every tree not only *occupies* a unique place but in effect *creates* that place—creates it by its very being-there and its becoming or constant metamorphosis. Such placement entails a decisive and unique arboreal ontology of place that is not the same as what obtains for ourselves or for other animal species—or for that matter, for rocks and other nonliving natural phenomena. We enter here into something quite remarkable: the singular *placeology* of trees. Other natural entities have their own peculiar mode of being implaced, but that with which we are concerned in this book is quite special.

We realize this specialness when we consider the case of a tree farm—where trees are planted in perfectly straight rows. Here there is an effort to impose a site-specific positionality upon the planting and growth of trees, sometimes for perfectly admirable purposes (such as reestablishing a forest that has been lost to logging). Yet, even if the seeds or saplings of the planted trees are at a determinate and repeated metric distance from each other—say, forty-five inches—the architectures of the branches and root systems of each developing tree will be unique: unique in their exact physical configuration, unique in their exposure to sun or contiguity with the soil, the precise ways by which they draw nutrients from the soil (in the case of a given tree and not just the *type of tree*, say a birch or an elm wherein there will be a certain convergence), and unique in the way the root system of a given tree interacts with that of another tree and the entire biome around it. The sitedness that determines the layout of the planted forest in its original format quickly gives way to a singularity of placement in the case of any given member of the growing forest.

One soon suspects that there is an intrinsic link between the growth pattern of a given tree and its unique placedness. The further along its growth—the more "mature" the tree is—the more its placiality takes on increasingly unique configurations. It is one thing to grow *as a type of tree*—here not only the metricality of positioning but also the speciated kind of tree do obtain—and quite another to grow as *this tree*: this member of this species. To be *this very tree* is tantamount to inhabiting *this very place*: setting forth its own way of having become placiated.

Such a place is not merely *a place in space*—as if space were a larger whole that contains particular places as so many determinate contents. The uniqueness of arboreal placedness is such that each tree *is* its own place, whatever its relation to a larger containment space (such as may be determined by a predesignated limit or border of a planted forest). Each growing tree not only *has a place*—as if it were to occupy a predesignated site—but, more radically, *it is a place*, the place that is indefeasibly its own and not that of any other. We are talking about a radical singularity here—where we recall that the word *radical* has for its etymon *radix*, i.e., "root." No wonder it is tempting to draw examples of placial singularity from the root-life of trees—even if the upper parts of trees are also unique in each and every case. The growth of any given tree is *from the ground up*, and it is in the ground that its roots reside even as its branches reach out and beyond the ground. The roots reside underground for the most part, even if certain root systems—e.g., that of the banyan tree—may also flourish above ground. But the exact positionality of roots considered as a matter of their exact spatial distribution is not what matters the most when it comes to placement.

What matters most is *arborescence*. By this term we refer to the animation, the ongoing growing life of trees, their becoming in time rather than their positionality in space. Mattering most is that the placedness of trees is a *becoming in time* that is not reducible to occupying a stretch of space—where "time" refers to the temporality of living process, that is, time as *undergone*, while "space" designates what is reducible to site and is subject to striation. In effect, time undergone is expressed in the very corporeity of trees—for instance, in the tree rings that register, in the annular fashion, patterns of the annual growth, all the way down to the nutrients a particular plant has received in any given year. We must come to see that the sense of place that characterizes the life of trees does not belong to sited space but is allied with time construed as ongoing process. Place can be said to manifest the *unhidden life of trees*—there where they show themselves becoming or leave material traces of such becoming. This is not just a becoming *in place* but a *becoming of place itself*: a placialization-in-time.

For place is not ever-the-same. It is always becoming, just as much if differently from that which becomes in it—or rather, as we've been arguing, *as it*. For place is not something constant but is continually evolving, ever different in ways that we can see as well as assess—and manipulate in ways that suit the human species all too readily. Just so a tree-in-place is ever altering, evolving within its own speciation, indeed *as* its speciation: where *speciation* refers not to the exemplification of a preestablished species but to the unique configuration of a member of that species, its *individuation*.

Philosophical readers will recognize that we are here headed toward the worldview of Bergson—except that he never took up place in any serious way, confining himself to the two exclusive categories of space and time. Yet place is a third way of becoming—completing the *triton genos*—which we must not overlook, especially when it comes to living organic phenomena such as plants that are not only phenomena but also living beings with worlds of their own.

III

Places and their occupation tend to be associated with either generosity or extreme egoism. Inherently generous, a place is an opening, within certain limits, welcoming whomever or whatever is in it. It *provides space*—living space—for occupants. Only by overwriting or overriding the hospitality of the place itself do I claim it for myself or cede it to others in actions that are intrinsically egoistic.

In his *Pensées*, Blaise Pascal hears in the words "my place in the sun" a primordial and still ongoing possessive appropriation of the earth: "*Mine thine*. 'This is my dog,' said these poor children. 'That is my place in the sun.' There is the origin and image of the usurpation of the whole earth (*l'image de usurpation de toute la terre*)."[3] The expression "my place in the sun" sounds particularly pertinent to plants, which receive a significant portion of their nourishment from solar energy in the process of photosynthesis. But, since Plato, and even before him in pre-Socratic thinkers and their ancient Egyptian sources, the sun has been seen as universal, generative, and generous excess; the claim one lays to one's place *in* it carves out an exclusive, private, and privative niche, into which no other is to be admitted—or, if so, with a price to pay. Do plants take their places in the sun *à la* Pascal? Do they first usurp the whole earth, as the fraught evolutionary and biological term *plant colonization of land* implies?

The remarkable thing is that by *taking* their places plants *give* place to other things. In their consumption or decay, they make room for and are succeeded by many other forms of life, indeed by the entire livable world. Covering the whole *earth*, they bring the *world* into existence: the world as we and other living creatures come to know it. This is the basis of a widespread sociality among plants and a concrete basis for human social life too, as spelled out in our chapter 4 on "The Shared Sociality of Trees."

The cryptic formula taking = giving violates all the rules of capitalist economy and of binary formal logic. It does not fit the framework of "zero-sum" games, where the recipients of advantages and benefits obtain these goods at the expense of those to whom they are denied. Nor does it correspond to a physicalistic model of occupation, according to which no two bodies may be found in the same place at the same time. How do plants overstep or outgrow such rules, frameworks, and models: all of which are based on a metaphysics of determinate presence? In a nutshell, as they take their places, plants do not do so to the exclusion of others but, magnet-like, draw insects, birds, and other animals, fungi, bacteria and other plants toward themselves, that is to say, toward the places they inhabit in a nonexclusive, nonexclusionary manner.

The place of this date palm I am looking at now is this one and no other, just as the tree itself is unmistakably this very one, its leafy crown towering over the grass and shrubs underneath and standing out between the bare branches of plane trees it is surrounded by. Unique, the date palm is uniquely welcoming, its hospitality being of a piece with the place where it grows: the tree gathers around and on itself the birds and the fruit flies who feed on its succulent fruit, the mosses and the lichens spreading over the lower part of its trunk, children running with happy shrieks around it, and myself as quietly admiring it. One way to think about such green hospitality is through the prism of the distinction between places, sites, and space. Although it provides nourishment for birds and insects, the date palm is much more than a useful or usable site; it is a living expression of its species and of the dynamic interaction of this particular vegetal being with its environment. And although it takes up space—in the sense that no other palm tree, plane tree, or shrub grows where it does—it convokes into being a place that was not there before. In effect, this might be one of the keys to the seemingly contradictory formula taking = giving: the *vegetal taking up of space is giving place*. This is place for growth and interaction but also for fading and dying: place both animated and animating, deanimated and deanimating, or reanimated otherwise.

The line of thinking we are pursuing here goes well beyond the question of occupation. To "take place" is not just to occupy a locale; it also means to happen, to occur. There is no event, there is no time, without something taking place. A tree takes place. A tree happens. The event of *this* date palm tree unfolds (grows, flourishes, blossoms, rots). And it happens in this very place, right here, where it grows, the place it cannot abandon without losing its being and identity. (A curious exception is yet another palm tree, the so-called stilt palm, *Verschaffeltia splendida*, which, while moving imperceptibly, nevertheless moves in the sense of locomotion; by growing new stilt-like roots, using them as support structures for the trunk, and abandoning old roots, it gets the chance to forage for light and resources in areas quite distant from the original site of its growth.) Just as much, the place of the tree cannot abandon this tree so long as the tree is in that place. If the tree withers away or is cut, the place will no longer be *of* this tree and its growth; it will no longer be that place at all; the logic of substitution applicable to abstract space simply does not apply in this case. The places of trees are temporally finite, even as they render possible the time, the eventmental aspect, of what is taking place in and as them.

IV

Trees often occupy the edges of our experience: as when we view a setting sun through a row of trees that serves as the outer edges of our visual field, providing its framing as it were. Similarly, if less dramatically, the trees that ring the yard of the house I inhabit constitute its de-lineation: "my property ends over there," we say, gesturing toward the trees that are situated at the edge of the plot on which we live. But even when trees are not on the outer edges of a landscape on which the sun is setting or at the limits of our own home property, they tend to be relegated to the outer edges of everyday experience, literally "marginalized" there and taken for granted. On closer inspection, however, we realize that trees actively populate many parts of our lives and precisely in their status as edges. Among these everyday situations are the following (and the reader can easily supply others):

> the intimate internal edges in a garden we have cultivated, variegating its contents and providing a characteristic configuration of the vegetal presence of the garden;
> the dense edges of a thick forest through which we are slowly making our way: edges that tell us much about the character and extent of that forest, even as it forecloses views of what lies beyond it;
> the tops of tall trees reaching into the sky, thereby marking the most elevated point of our visual field; no wonder Avicenna could consider such upward positionality as demonstrating the existence of a vegetal soul that moves against nature within nature.

In these various ways and countless others, trees act to *give edge* to our ongoing experience: to give to it a characteristic contour, to delimit its extent, to suggest, to foreshadow, and at the same time to foreclose what lies beyond it and to populate it with edges integral to the space where we are now standing or walking or otherwise moving about in our ongoing life-worlds. Trees are edge-donative, lending their variegated edges so as to give shape and specificity to wherever we or other, nonhuman living beings may happen to be, whether high up or low down or somewhere in the middle. We appreciate the presence of trees all the more when we are in circumstances where there are no trees at all: such as when we are at sea or in a desert wholly devoid of trees. Then the horizon comes to the fore and is thematized as such.

Speaking of a horizon, a place arguably entails irreducible broadness, the spread or the spreading out, which—not necessarily of a geometrical or geographical order—is capacious enough for existence, notably for a settled form of existence. Greek (*plateia, platys*) and Roman (*platea*) etymologies of "place" point in this direction. At the same time, there is the category *plant*, in which differences between flowers and mosses, annual and perennial varieties, trees and grasses, are flattened. And, besides this epistemic flattening, *plant* also involves an ontic (if not an ontological) and practical flattening, the leveling of the earth in an attempt to create the places of crop cultivation that are at the root of humanly habitable places. While trees, particularly the fructiferous varieties and those used as timber, are also subject to cultivation, they undermine the different modes of flattening inherent in planthood. The verticality of trees, like that of high mountains, implicitly forbids human habitation while welcoming plenty of birds, insects, and other animals. And this is not to mention how the dense and tall arboreal community of the forest hides the horizon from view, rendering the phenomenological notion of experience itself unworkable and, perhaps, in so doing, inviting fresh elaborations of a *horizonless* experience that takes its bearings from the places of the trees themselves. Although Heidegger has already pointed in this direction with his notion of *Lichtung,* or "clearing," there is still much to do with respect to a phenomenology of trees and their places.

Trees not only provide edges to what we experience around us. They have *their own edges*: edges of the branches that spread out from the trunk of a given tree; of the trunk itself; and in the roots of trees, however invisible these may be if fully buried. Such edges are not just outer, as are those of the examples we have just discussed. They may also be inner—located within the trees themselves: in the bark, in the pulp of the trunk, inside roots and tubers. These internal edges are everywhere in trees, even if we overlook them when we are taken by the more conspicuous edges of the tree as a whole (as very early in the morning when the sun illuminates a certain tree, bringing it into the light).

Every tree possesses a congeries of edges—themselves of multiple kinds and sizes even in the case of a single tree, ranging from the enormity of a redwood tree we confront to the tiny tips of the bristles on a low-lying conifer. All such edges configurate in unique patterns—unique to the species of a given tree but also accruing to that tree as it makes its way to full growth, which is never quite complete in the teleological sense of the term. Trees are intensely edge-bearing: *bearing edges out* in unique patterns that catch our eye and *holding them in* by way of patterns that we can sometimes touch more easily than we can see as such. Many of these patterns are in accordance with "modular growth"— growth that reiterates a basic "module" and reconfigures it in ever-new combinations. But the edges of the same module positioned differently are never quite the same. This is the vegetal version of what Edmund Husserl called "free variation in imagination." But we are talking about a free variation *in perception* that occurs when we find ourselves in the presence of trees, and the variation is not in the presentation of an eidos as it is for Husserl; we have to do with the variation of a given module, itself interacting with the environmental conditions and the rest of the place it is found in.

Tree edges can serve both as borders and as boundaries in the distinction we pursued earlier. They are the former when they are situated at certain precise locations in a formal garden, as when a straight row of carefully cultivated trees is planted to delimit a given avenue, as in Le Nôtre's garden at Versailles. Such trees constitute a definite chartable space. In other cases, such as British gardens (and most casually constructed home gardens), the edges furnished by trees are irregular and easily traversible: construed as a single cluster, such edges amount to boundaries as permeable edges. Borders and boundaries are usually associated with the mapping of national or state territories, but both forms of edging can create configurational limits in many other contexts, as with the moving forests that figure into certain of Shakespeare's plays and that furnish imagined perimeters to human interactions.

Not only do trees have inherent and highly diverse edges, but so do the *places* of trees: all such places have characteristic edges of which we are at least dimly aware as we stand on the ground these places occupy. Such places are composed of porous edges that can be permeated by various fluids or traversed by mobile animals (including ourselves), thereby replicating the osmotic mechanisms by which a plant draws water and other nutrients from the soil. A tree cannot move itself over the already existing edge of its own place, but the edges of trees themselves move, expanding or contracting in keeping with the seasons, the phase of growth, and other such factors. A tree also sends essentially detachable parts of itself well beyond its own literal edge and stable place in the shape of seeds or pollen—not to mention leaves that are equally fecund since they decay into the soil and replenish it. The edges of trees are themselves mobile, with their movements occurring as growth, decay, or metamorphosis (these being the three types of motion, in addition to locomotion, recognized by Aristotle)—all this happening within its own given place.

In short, the edges of a tree distend *all over its own place*. This place, which we are approaching from several perspectives in this book, is itself comparatively stationary. For this is the place of a given tree—or a cluster of trees—and to count as *that* place, *the* place of *this* tree or group of trees, it has to be edged in certain perceptible ways. These ways create a unique pattern for that of which they together constitute the place: no two arboreal places are ever just the same but differ significantly from tree to tree, each tree not only calling for its own place but *creating* that place, *being* its place. Moreover, no one tree is ever the same as itself if we consider various time scales that obtain for seasonal changes as well as for the growth and decay of that tree in a given place.

Such complex singularity of placement distinguishes the situation of trees from that of built or constructed ways of being-in-place: ways that vary from city blocks to the foundations of houses, to country roads and highways, bookcases to kitchen cabinets. Each of these diverse things brings with it its own characteristic and largely predetermined place, usually created in keeping with a definable use or purpose that calls for a particular mode of placement that is comparatively easy to replicate: a standing bookcase with its inset rows, a road that can support heavy vehicles, etc. But trees cannot be said to have any such definite, replicable pattern of emplacement. If there are patterns at all, they are not replicated in the delimited forms assumed by the places of what is ready-to-hand for human utilization.

Each tree, as well as each type of tree, has its own way of being-in-place.

V

We are arguing that trees, indeed each and every tree, has a place of its own. Again we must ask: how are we to understand such a place? To begin with, it will be located on the earth and in the earth:

> *on the earth* considered as a material basis from which a given tree arises: this is what we conventionally call "the ground," and it is composed of soil with all that this contains by way of ancillary forms of life: worms, fungi, etc., as well as nonliving things such as rocks;
>
> *in the earth*: trees are not stationed on the surface of the earth like Christmas trees propped up in living rooms, they go down into it, thanks to their root systems; this is not only a matter of descent but of active engagement with the earth itself—with and in its soil and whatever it contains, living or not; it is a matter of an active immersion in that very place.

From what we have just been saying, one major claim emerges. This is that the placement of trees always occurs in an *edge-to-edge pattern*, a pattern that is as pervasive as it is multiple. Trees are not isolated entities that live autonomous, self-sufficient lives but rather beings—events as much as entities—that subsist only by living from edge to edge. These edges proliferate even as they diminish periodically.[4] The most elaborate such interedged existence is found underground, where trees communicate with each other and across species and biological kingdoms through entire networks of connective forces: forces that include bacteria and other microorganisms that convey a variety of tacit messages from one tree to another. Trees live edge-to-edge underground. But they communicate at their upper edges as well, given that the leaves of trees are now known to pass on information from one tree to others near it via airborne biochemicals. What is transmitted is not only information in the usual sense of the term as referring to something quantified and coded: we are speaking of qualitative sensory messages that animate an entire world of *e-co-affectivity* in Marjolein Oele's apt term, a world that consists in a myriad of "interfaces" that constitute entire ecoworlds, whether above or below the ground.[5] This can also be characterized as a world in which *ecoproprioception* (in George Quasha's suggestive word) is the animating force: whereby an organism reaches out to an entire environment and comes to know it by way of diverse sensory systems.[6]

The proliferation of edges plays a very important role in a plant's survival. Like all sessile beings, plants are literally tethered to the places where they grow, which means that in a situation of danger (an attack by herbivorous animals or insects, etc.), they cannot flee from that place. It is, therefore, of utmost importance for a plant, whether it is a tree or not, to continuously monitor the fluid situation in its vicinity in order to pick up the slightest signals of impending threats, which would allow it to activate various physiological defense mechanisms. This is quite established in plant science, but what purpose do the edges of plants serve? Our response is that the more multifaceted the living edges of plants (leaves, branches, but also brachiated roots), the more sensitive they can be to whatever is going on in the places of their growth. Trees, indeed, present some of the most multifaceted living edges among all other plants, such as grasses or flowers. A slightly different angle and position of apparently replicated, redundant structures (modules) afford them such increased sensitivity. It is like an incredibly complex construction of a 3-D model of the place they are in, a model that is not "ideal" (it is neither a blueprint nor anything like eidos) but is of a piece with the place itself, inherent in it.

In sum, in exploring the place(s) of trees in particular, we are talking about how trees link up at their edges—how they interface with the soil and the atmosphere as well as with other trees and certain plants as well. It is a matter of existing edge-to-edge. With trees we are into an edge world—a world altogether, and in countless ways, on edge.[7]

VI

The variegated directionalities of growth in trees are vivid instantiations of phenomenological intentionality in the vegetal world, a directedness-toward that, according to Husserl, constitutes the basic dynamic structure of human consciousness. The place of a tree is a knot into which these arboreal directionalities are tied. In this book, we attempt not so much to disentangle this knot as to follow some of its many twists and turns, complications and coimplications.

Branches of trees have a way of reaching out in a quasi-protentional manner, exceeding themselves as it were. It is tempting to regard them as intentionally arrayed: seeking sunlight, proffering leaves, *there for a purpose*. Vegetal *branching out* bears, in effect, on a middle region between earth and sky in a tentacular manner. One of us (EC) cherishes a very early memory of being drawn to depict tree branches as a challenging and exhilarating task for a fledgling artist of eight years old. This memory is preserved in an early painting that is a study of the arboreal branching of a very large tree. "I was quite aware of the massive trunk that anchored the tree, but I was much more struck by the exfoliation of the branches. Taken together, trunk and branches—and the roots beneath—established a unique place on that college campus in Topeka that I could still locate today after many years of absence." (We return to this experience in our discussion of "plants from afar" in interlude 3.)

The other coauthor (MM) often reminisces about a tall birch tree that grew in front of the apartment complex in Moscow, Russia, where he lived together with his parents as a child. "Whether bare in wintertime or covered with earring-like catkins and leaves in spring and summer, gently swaying birch branches invariably greeted me whenever I glanced out the window. It was as though the branches led a life of their own, independent of the trunk and the roots, their elegant, pliable yet sturdy, extensions faithfully facing me whenever I turned their way." Could it be that children are more attuned to the middle region of branching-out that trees, among other kinds of plants, call forth into being? If so, are children (not forgetting the child within each adult) more in tune with the intensities of existence that wells up in and as the middle—a middle expressly valorized by Deleuze and Guattari?

Many trees are inherently *tentacular*, as if equipped with their own arms, extending into the sunlight and the open air, sometimes seeming to exude an expressivity that is all their own. Their brachiated being contrasts starkly with certain types of roots, such as bulbs and other tuberous roots, which tend to turn in upon themselves as if seeking obscurity. Instead of turning *out*, as with branches, they turn *in*—in upon themselves. And they accomplish this in-volution characteristically *in the earth*. The up-here-above of branches stands in stark contrast with the down-there-below of tuberous roots.

Based on this difference, we can discern two basic kinds of place that trees occupy and/or create: two expressions of the process of arboreal placialization. One is open-ended and outward-going, mitotic, as it were—self-differentiating at every phase. This yields place as *ramified*. The other is closed-down and inward-tending, coalescing rather than exfoliating, consolidating rather than thinning-out. This is place as *amalgamating*. Trees offer both kinds of places; more than this, they *are* both—and both at once.

Each kind of place is essential; together they are coessential. There is no tree that does not have elements of both; indeed, that *is both*. How is this so? It is by a process of self-differentiation whereby trees not only grow upward and downward, placializing themselves in these two primary avatars—each of which carries with it characteristic kinds of growth and, depending on the species of a given tree, peculiar modes of place. Two primary *kinds* of place result from the exfoliation of trees: arboreal and terraceous, each with its own modes of variation. On the one hand, as arboreal trees placialize themselves in a primarily *outwardizing* direction; on the other hand, as terraceous they become placial in a mainly *inwardizing* tendency.

To these two primary placializations of trees must be added a third: *lateralizing*. For trees grow not only up but *out*—out to the side. The result is a peculiar kind of sidewise place that realizes a third directionality: a way *around*: around a central trunk or, in the case of trees with multiple trunks, circling them as in a loosely fitting girdle or garland of placiality. In this respect, one of us cannot help but think of a three-hundred-year-old prickly juniper tree growing in the Príncipe Real Garden in Lisbon, Portugal (figure 3.1).

While the tree itself is seven meters tall, its sprawling branches, supported by a meshwork of inserted columns and horizontal

Figure 3.1. Old juniper tree, Príncipe Real Garden, Lisbon, Portugal. Photograph on-site by M. Marder, May 7, 2022.

bars, reach the length of fifteen meters in all directions. A welcome refuge from the scorching sun in the summer, the extended place of this tree is the public square that emerged around and under it—thanks, precisely, to its lateralizing growth.

Such arboreal mid-regions are often less conspicuous than the upper parts (i.e, the "crown") or, by inference, the lower parts (the "anchor"), but they are no less vital to the overall placiality of trees. For trees invite circumnavigation—if not by our moving body, then by our circulating look, which often follows the midriff placiality with as much interest as the upward moving branches or the downward-tending roots.

In plant science, too, the middle gains significance. Think of a seed, for instance. On the verge of germinating, it is the middle that stretches in two or more directions at once; otherwise, it would not have been a middle. In the course of stretching out, elongating, exiting the enclosure of a point, which is far from fixed, it calls into being the extremes it spans and many other midpoints (in fact, an infinite number of them) between these extremes. Beyond any objective measures, the distance in between is vital space, the field of existence, the place of plants. The spans of the middle are the times of plant life. In the middle, all referents are too dynamic to warrant any certainty, expanding and contracting, growing and decaying, uncoiling, recoiling, metamorphosing. The end and the beginning, at which these vegetal activities are arbitrarily cut short, give off the appearance of a polar opposition. But they too are variations on the middle. Polarity is the residue of a middle that has undergone oppositional growth and that, in its sway, has assigned their respective meanings and places to antipodean positions.

The directionality of trees is thus threefold: up-and-out, around-and-about, and downward-going. These are not three strictly separate vectors of a tree but three modes of its placial animation in which the placialities overlap and sometimes merge at their edges: so much so that we rarely bother to distinguish them as separate parts but take them in as one continuous flow of being-in-place. To regard them as discrete parts would be to spatialize them unduly—whereas we are arguing that place occurs as a process, as something ongoing and ever changing, something happening not just in time but *as time: lived time.*

To regard the disposition of these three parts as "triaxial"—however tempting this may be—is to overly objectify them. We must resist this temptation. Even to talk, as we have ourselves, of three *regions* or *directionalities* of arboreal placement is to invoke terms that are spatial rather than properly placial in character. It is to come from the outside of arboreal placement rather than doing justice to the way that trees configure themselves from within: in place rather than in space. The challenge is to do justice to the intrinsic and quite unique placedness of trees themselves. How are we to find the language for the way in which they exist placially—and how may we resist the strong impulse to convert this *how* of placialization into the *what* of settled spatial terms such as *axial* or *dimensional* or any of a number of other such spatially overdetermined terms, tempting as it may be to invoke them (as we have just done ourselves)?

It is a matter of doing justice to the flowing of place rather than its stabilization, much less its quantification: a flowing that is a *becoming*: becoming as a variant of itself through placial proliferation. This is not to deny that there are certain basic discernible tendencies in the life of a given tree—tendencies that allow us to apprehend them in place and as place. When one writes about place in the dynamic sense we endorse, the very language one is drawn to use is overdetermined and predetermined by a spatial sensibility that has virtues of economy and elegance, but one that fails to capture the uniquely configured, frequently very dense, and always complex placiality of trees themselves. This placiality is always in process of becoming.

Interlude 2

PLANTS UP-CLOSE: THE CASE OF MOSS

In July 2018, desperate to escape from unbearable summer heat, one of the authors (MM) went with his then two-year-old son on an impromptu weeklong vacation in the region of Sintra, just outside of Lisbon, Portugal. Sintra is a lush mountainous area, very close to the westernmost point of continental Europe, an area boasting its own humid and cool microclimate. During the long walks on winding forest paths and small mountain roads, the toddler immediately learned a new word he would often repeat throughout the stay in Sintra and thereafter: *moss*. Indeed, moss was everywhere, covering with its thick carpet roadside stone fences, tree trunks, and boulders scattered on the forest floor. Touching its humid green softness with the open palm of his hand, MM's son would savor as much the experience as the word itself, repeating the gesture and uttering it over and over. In the child's mind, the entire place was linked to the ubiquitous tiny plant he had encountered for the first time there. Regardless of an astonishing variety of trees and other plants growing in Sintra, for him it was *a place of moss* (figure int2.1).

Such fascination is foreign to most philosophers who, habitually neglecting plants, pay no attention whatsoever to the

Figure int2.1. Moss in Sintra, Portugal. Photograph on-site by M. Marder, December 22, 2022.

smallest among them. Plant nature in general and mosses in particular are beneath them, those lofty thinkers refusing to bend, to stoop, physically or spiritually, as low as that. One salient exception is Rousseau, quipping in his *Reveries of a Solitary Walker*: "They say a German once wrote a book about a lemon-skin. I could have written one about every grass in the meadows, every moss in the woods, every lichen covering the rocks—and I didn't want to leave even one blade of grass or atom of vegetation without a full and detailed description."[1] On Rousseau's reading, behind the most careful naturalistic observations and reflections, we are likely not to find the ideal of scholarly detachment but passionate commitment, a child's wonder and curiosity preserved throughout one's life and triggered, precisely, by "every grass in the meadows, every moss in the woods, every lichen covering the rocks." It is an excess of enthusiasm that borders on the impossible: to describe the tiniest bit, every "atom of vegetation" with praiseful admiration.

The father of modern scientific method, aspiring to smash the so-called idols of the mind, Francis Bacon did study mosses, which, together with mushrooms, he considered to be "imperfect plants."[2] If his studies are interesting, they are so not for what they reveal about moss, but, on the contrary, for what they say by omission and despite themselves, unconsciously, as it were. For example, Bacon insists that the "moss of trees is a kind of hair; for it is the juice of the tree that is excerned, and doth not assimilate."[3] Obviously, he omits the fact that moss can grow on rocks, where the theory that it consists of the exuded and unassimilated "juice" of a host plant makes little sense. And yet, in this glaring oversight, there is a glimmer of insight, an inadvertent admission that moss, as this unique plant and as a condensation of the flora in the miniature, is unassimilable for metaphysical thought. It is this relation of the unassimilable that we propose to examine up close.

According to Bacon's theory of juicy exuding, older plants grow more moss because their vigor is diminished, their sap unable to permeate the entire tree: "Old trees are more mossy far than young; for that the sap is not so frank as to rise all to the boughs, but tireth by the way and put out moss."[4] The emergence of moss is linked to stagnation, the diminished quality of plant metabolism that results in the exteriorization of the unassimilable portion of tree sap.

Bacon is not alone in thinking that moss (which also grows exuberantly on fallen tree trunks and branches) is a sign of decline in vegetal vigor. Hildegard von Bingen writes in her *Physica*: "When trees grow old, they begin to lose their inner greenness (*viriditas*), and if they are not young, they send the greenness and health, which they ought to have inside, to the exterior bark. Thus, moss grows on the bark because these trees do not have inner greenness."[5] Moss prompts a spatial confusion between what is (or should be) inside and what is (or should be) outside: it literally turns vigor inside out: externalized, vigor is implanted on the bark instead of circulating in the tree. While consisting of "greenness and health," linked to the places it covers, moss expresses their weakening in the host. In effect, neither Bacon nor Hildegard before him acknowledge the host as host, since they do not see in moss a parasitic plant living on a plant of another species, but part of the same plant, just situated on the wrong side of things, as far as proper metabolic activity is concerned. The view of moss as internally unassimilable conceals the gap between the same and the other, actually assimilating the symbiont to the host.

Colloquially speaking, "gathering moss" is growing old. As an old Latin proverb goes, "A rolling stone gathers no moss" (*Saxum volutum non obducitur musco*). While, in its initial sense, the dictum criticized those who, rootless and roaming the earth, assumed no responsibilities, according to a modern interpretation (picked up by Bob Dylan in the song "Like a Rolling Stone" and by a British rock band in their very name, "The Rolling Stones"), it meant that, being in constant motion, one escaped the states of stagnation and senescence, if not the sessility characteristic of plants. The historical shift in the interpretation of the proverb is worth considering. For the ancients, the contrast is not between rest and motion but between kinds of movement: the purely mechanical, relatively fast displacement of a stone, on the one hand, and the self-directed, relatively slow movement of vegetal growth, on the other. More than that, with varying degrees of approval, the proverb describes a situation where strict dividing lines are maintained between the inorganic realm and the organicity of moss. A rolling stone refuses the community—indeed, an entire world—that moss could have created on its surface. All the same, moss remains unassimilable to a narrow vision of movement and to an order built on the need to compartmentalize various kinds of being.

Perhaps the most remarkable piece of evidence for how unassimilable moss is to metaphysical thought is its unique temporality. Just as it confounds the distinction between the inside and the outside of vitality, so it muddles the difference between youth and old age, the before and the after of vegetal life. With moss, the bookends of plant history close into a circle: "the most primitive of land plants,"[6] one of the vegetal pioneers preparing the ground for future growth,[7] it thrives on nearly lifeless or entirely dead trees. Softening not only the sharp outlines of rocks and leafless branches but also the edges of time—those abruptly dropping cliffs of the beginning and the end—moss escapes the power of linear chronologies and hierarchies. Anarchic, it performs the work of time, grinding down rocks, speeding up the decay of fallen tree trunks, metabolizing mineral and vegetal matter. As Robin Wall Kimmerer puts it: "The rocks are beyond slow, beyond strong, and yet yielding to a soft green breath as powerful as a glacier, the mosses wearing away their surfaces, grain by grain bringing them slowly back to sand. There is an ancient conversation going on between mosses and rocks, poetry to be sure."[8] We may add that the conversation, too, is beyond ancient: it is that of time itself in its two modes of the mutable and the immutable, a "moving image of eternity," as Plato put it so memorably.

Why is our conceptualization of time, drawing on metaphysical order and stability, ineffectual when it comes to the time of moss? First, as we have seen, the relative terms *young* and *old*, *before* and *after*, are inapplicable there where a linear chronology breaks down. Second, the paradigm of energy gradually dissipating in the measure of distancing from an energetically rich beginning no longer works when faced with moss: diminished vitality coincides with the exuberance of mossy vegetal life, one that infinitely mirrors and is mirrored in "the architecture of the surrounding forest."[9] Third, though "primitive," moss encompasses at least fourteen thousand species and includes virtually all methods of plant reproduction (be they sexual or asexual) and growth, reliant on mutual interactions with the boundary layer or the microclimate that surrounds each leaf and growing point of every plant. Hence, already in the nineteenth century, a relevant entry in *The Edinburgh Encyclopaedia* stated: "He who could examine the nutrition, the growth, the regular confirmation, the provision made for the continuation of the species ... of even the minutest Phascum [mosses], without perceiving in them proofs of intelligence, power, and goodness, would probably receive no more conviction from the sublimest truths that astronomy can unfold."[10] Finally, moss grinds rocks to sand and builds up the soil for future plant growth; it performs simultaneously the tasks of analysis and synthesis, complicating the (mythical) image of time as a universal destroyer, the merciless devourer of all without exception.

As for the philosophers' relation to moss, it would be fair to conclude that, even in the best of cases, this plant remains inassimilable to their thought, which it nonetheless stimulates and props up from the outside. Let's refer to Rousseau once again and pair him with Friedrich Nietzsche's Zarathustra. The Genevan philosopher recalls reaching a patch of wilderness in the mountains of the Môtiers region that left him speechless. "Gradually succumbing to the powerful impression of my surroundings," he relates, "I forgot about botany and plants, sat down on pillows of *lycopodium* and mosses, and began dreaming to my heart's content, imagining that I was in a sanctuary unknown to the whole universe."[11]

Besides furnishing a pillow that supports Rousseau's body, mosses are the strange plants that make him "forget about botany and plants." What sort of oblivion is that? The pairing of the forgotten plants with botany is revealing: Rousseau cleanses from his mind plants as objects of botanical study arranged in systems of strict classification. The "sanctuary unknown" he imagines himself to be in is another relation to vegetal life not mediated by such scientific constructs. The dreamy state, in which Rousseau immerses himself—the state that marks his reveries—is that of a forgetting that ultimately *recalls something else* outside the sphere of conscious representation, namely a togetherness with plants. Plunging into the deep reserves of the unconscious, he reconnects with the sources whence his philosophy springs. And all this is occasioned by moss that, despite not having roots (it only has rhizoids), despite not burrowing deep into the dark of the earth, which could epitomize the unconscious, induces rapture and claims for itself the philosopher, body and soul—the body seated on its soft pillows and the soul experiencing the sway of its powerful impressions.

Nietzsche's Zarathustra also dreams (and, indeed, sleeps) on moss. He lies down on a bed of moss under a tree in a period of transition, when he realizes that he needs living companions, not dead ones: "Zarathustra found himself in a deep forest, and he did not see a path anywhere. So he laid the dead man into a hollow tree—for he wanted to protect him from the wolves—and he himself lay down on the ground and the moss, his head under the tree. And soon he fell asleep, his body weary but his soul unmoved."[12] Rousseau sat on pillows of moss; for Zarathustra, mossy ground becomes the support for his prone body, his head slotted between plants: the moss below him and the tree above. Without a path in the dark of a forest, Zarathustra finds a way in his own unconscious, in sleep facilitated by moss. Waking up rejuvenated, he utters his famous speech "High Noon," addressing the living and refusing to speak to and for the dead (who nevertheless feed the growth of the living with their very decomposition). From below, moss bolsters and refreshes his thought and his relation to life, producing an effect that is diametrically opposed to the loss of vigor with which it had been associated by Bacon and even by Hildegard. Unassimilable, mentioned but in passing in the narrative of Zarathustra's sleep and awakening, moss secretly prepares the moment of high noon, of another enlightenment and the shortest shadows.

To return to Sintra and to MM son's first experience with moss, what was stunning (if also in line with the way children tend to think) was that he applied this word he had just learned to the place where he first encountered it, to all tiny plants, to the trimmed grass of lawns, to lichens. And so, in his mind, moss became a metonym of Sintra, even as it was easily assimilated and extended to the category *small growing things*. We should note, however, that it was in this way assimilable to a world seen through a child's eyes, which is, at the same time, the world unassimilable to the presumably self-sufficient adult experience of those who, at Kant's urging, have emerged from their "self-incurred immaturity." The category *small growing things*, as it germinates in this experience, is not abstract but both anchored in a certain place, from which it is indissociable, and given a certain shape—figured as moss. Its concrete universality, to resort to Hegel's term, is highly significant, above all as an alternative manner of approaching plant life.

In their turn, Rousseau's reveries and the enlightenment of Nietzsche's Zarathustra try to recover a child's wonder, the point of view that, in this case, *identifies with* and *recognizes itself in* small growing things. Instead of advocating on behalf of adult seriousness, one should appeal to that immaturity which is of a piece with the promise of life, with life's own essential unripeness and playful puerility. Within that jovial scheme, calling all small growing things *moss* is not a mistake, lumping them together into one and the same "basket;" rather, it is giving something like a proper name to a category, rendered singular thanks to this name, the experience it betokens, and the place where it has been encountered. The apparent disorder among levels of generality that ensues is, actually, a different order, attentive to moss's unassimilability, its irreducibility to the taxonomic division (or the phylum) Bryophyta within the kingdom Plantae.

We say that things gather moss when they grow old, unless they—like a rolling stone—maintain themselves in motion. But here it is moss that gathers diverse beings irrespective of their formal classifications and, overcoming the segregation ingrained right into our "mature" cognition, rejuvenates thinking. This is what MM discovered in Sintra with his son's help. This is what we have just rediscovered in Rousseau and Nietzsche. And this is what we will keep finding out in varied forays into the philosophy of vegetal life.

We are now at a midpoint of our book, which may be approached otherwise from the in-between perspective of the interludes. In the first interlude, we focused on the place-bound mode of thinking, which, while practiced and honed by plants, has the potential to enrich the understanding of human cognition. In this second interlude, we have been exploring the ramifying meanings and connotations of one particular plant—moss—as it is experienced close-up: as close as it was felt to be to a child's hand going over its soft surface or Zarathustra's body recumbent on it. In the third and final interlude, we shall consider how plants fare in situations where their presence is most fully appreciated when presented and savored at a certain distance. This is the distance embodied in their depicted presence in paintings in which plant life figures prominently.

4

THE SHARED SOCIALITY OF TREES, WITH IMPLICATIONS FOR PLACE

We next take up the phenomenon of the sociality of trees, a topic that is receiving increasing attention in recent times. Such sociality is the focus of section A in this chapter. In section B, we discuss the more general role of place and emplacement in the life of trees taken both individually and as living in their own unique societies. We here concentrate on trees as especially telling for issues of emplacement, but much of what we say about trees holds true for plants more generally.

A. ARBOREAL SOCIALITY: HOSPITALITY AND THE SHARED SOCIAL LIFE OF TREES

By "shared sociality" we do not mean anything quite like human *socializing*. Trees do not have formal greetings for each other, nor do they bow and courtesy; they do not make pleasant talk either—even if we may detect inarticulate equivalents of these highly civilized activities: a gust of wind blows through one tree and then ruffles its neighbor; they do not speak to one another in so many words, but they do make creaking sounds that seem almost protolinguistic even if there is no settled syntax or shared vocables.

What we do mean by shared sociality can be described by reference to three factors: arboreal hospitality, communication, and community-as-commons. Let us say a word about each of these basic ways in which trees can be said to enter into a social relationship.

Arboreal Hospitality. Trees are hosts to many species of life other than their own. As I sit on my porch, I (EC) cannot help but note small flocks of local sparrows, intermittently alighting in the trees in the garden before me, lingering there briefly whether singly or in small groups of three or four. They are clearly feeling *welcome* in the branches or they wouldn't be flying onto them so eagerly and energetically. In its material articulation, their being-together-with-each-other is made possible by tree limbs. If not *offered* in any formally recognizable sense, such hospitality is nevertheless provided by the perches that populate the numerous trunks and branches of trees. The birds recognize them as perchable at a glance: prolonged scrutiny is not called for—as it might be, for instance, if the same birds were looking for a viable place for building a nest. Otherwise, a quick look suffices—as it does for humans who seek a safe spot to land while hang gliding.[1]

Of course, birds also find perches in low-lying bushes and on lawns, but there is something especially enticing about branches and limbs in the midsections and crowns of trees—as if these yield temporary homes: homes away from whatever more settled homes the same birds inhabit. In such places, nests are not required, just familiar habitats in bushes or trees with which they are already acquainted. In addition to being momentary perches, these habitats can also offer settled protection both overnight and from inclement weather if there is no safe way to return to their original home-place. The exact locations of such habitats are often difficult for humans to detect, hidden as they often are when viewed from the ground. But we can be assured that they are *up there* or *out there* in the trees somewhere, offering an ongoing tacit hospitality, which, unlike a cave or a lair with its circumscribed entrance, allows for easy settling-into in diverse circumstances.

Beyond birds being offered such arboreal hospitality, something comparable happens with many other species of animals—ranging from humans who take shelter under trees, whether from a need for rest or a place to read, to do meditation, or even to paint (as one of us, EC, has done since childhood), to dogs who "lie in wait" and gophers who tunnel into the soil next to a tree. But all such ways of taking advantage of the hospitality that trees offer aboveground are outnumbered by the ways that trees provide an occasion for the flourishing of bacteria, among other microorganisms, or fungi that cluster at their base and infiltrate their root systems, their trunks, and extend all the way up to their upper branches and leaves. Merlin Sheldrake's recent book *Entangled Life* describes the myriad ways in which trees are "socially networked by fungi"—fungi that "stitch worlds together."[2] This happens in myriad ways, each of which can be considered a form of the *in*-habitation of trees by fungi: living as fungi do underground amid tree roots and on the trunks and limbs of trees in countless ways. This is an extraordinary form of arboreal hospitality that is normally invisible to the naked eye.

Ecologist Suzanne Simard coined the telling phrase "wood wide web."[3] She recalls her experience as a graduate student in ecology:

> In pulling back the forest floor using microscopic and genetic tools, I discovered that the vast below ground mycelial network

is a bustling community of mycorrhizal fungal species. These fungi are *mutualistic*. They connect the trees with the soil in a market exchange of carbon and nutrients and link the roots of paper birches and Douglas firs in a busy, cooperative Internet. . . . The trees were communicating through the web![4]

Notice here especially the italicized word *mutualistic*. Its minimal sense is that of a two-way interaction—and, when it comes to fungi, more than two-way. In the latter case, we have to do with vastly multiple ways in which the fate of trees is linked with that of fungi, themselves multiple in kind and type. As Sheldrake details it, fungi flourish not just as individual organisms but in and with the presence of trees, whether literally inside them, under them, alongside them, or dangling down from them. It is a matter of *symbiosis*: two basic kinds of life, arboreal and fungal, living together and dependent on each other.

The term *symbiosis* was coined in 1877 by German botanist Albert Frank; symbiosis refers to "the living together of fungal and algal partners."[5] Very telling in this respect is the Greek prefix of the term, *sym* (with), which renders sym-biosis as with-living or living-with. Life is, actually, inconceivable without such basic withness, whether it is the life of symbiotic organisms, as formally and scientifically recognized, or indeed of all other biological beings. It is the *withness* of collusion and collision alike. Plants, including trees, live and proliferate so vigorously and intensely because they embody and practice the withness of life itself. They cohabit *in* (they co-in-habit) the world, which comes into existence thanks to the cohabitats that they create and occupy, tenaciously holding onto them as integral parts of who they are, at the same time actively inhabiting the elements of air, water, earth, and solar fire; other forms of life; and what remains of the dead.

Additionally, more than just two kinds of life are at stake; often conjoined with them are lichens—a frequent third partner that further complicates the picture. In short, it is a matter of multiplicity feeding upon multiplicity: multiplicity galore! As Sheldrake puts it: "life is nested biomes all the way down."[6] All of this can be considered a situation of highly ramified mutual hospitality on the part of trees acting as hosts to fungi and lichen—and of these latter to the trees themselves. Such shared hospitality is a key form of the many ways in which trees and other plants provide a welcoming reception while being themselves welcomed into the world of living beings.

In these manifold ways and still others, trees actively convey a message of open hospitality. They communicate both explicitly and implicitly that they are open to being inhabited or at least visited by other living things. In this regard, they *have something to say to one another.* They do not say it in words, but they pass messages along among themselves (including those of biochemical variety), messages that convey openness to being influenced as well as offering shelter: each being a form of hospitality to others in their midst, whether this other is a tree of the same or another species, a bird, an insect, a fungus, or a human being. The porosity and outright permeability to each other of distinct kinds of existences, despite being set apart in Western systems of classification, is both the ground and the outcome of this profound *ontological* hospitality of plants.

Communication. Intrinsic to offering hospitality is communicating receptivity to the visitor: if not in so many words, then by gestures. Trees are not just in touch with each other, through the intermingling of their boughs and limbs in closely forested regions, but also with intricate fungal, bacterial, and rhizomatic webworks on and under the ground which they share.

Arboreal hospitality is most intricately effected through communication between fungal and bacterial networks. As Simard states it: "These discoveries [of symbiotic underground networks] have transformed our understanding of trees from competitive crusaders of the self to members of a connected, relating, communicating system."[7] We have here a living paradox: trees, arguably the most stalwart living beings we experience on earth, are not self-sufficing. They offer hospitality to other species, but they are themselves deeply dependent beings—dependent upon elemental presences above, around, and under them: ultimately, the sun as the source of energy and the earth as a reservoir of nutrients, which they, to be sure, replenish.

Trees are also dependent on something not known or even suspected until relatively recently: relationships with neighboring trees through fungal networks as transmitters of vital messages. These networks, termed *mycelia*, are webs that can extend for many miles: one in Oregon extends for two thousand acres. Such mycelia are the very fabric of the social life of trees. As Peter Wohlleben puts it:

> The two partners work together. The fungus not only penetrates and envelops the tree's roots, but also allows its web to roam through the surrounding forest floor. In so doing, it extends the roots of a tree's own roots as the web extends to other trees. Here, it connects with other trees' fungal partners and roots. And so a network is created, and now it's easy for the trees to exchange vital nutrients [in fending off invasion] . . . such as an impending insect attack.[8]

Here the fungal network acts to *alert* trees that might otherwise be clueless about the insect attack. Besides the biochemical signals that serve this purpose, Wohlleben speculates that there is something like a reward system at play: "in exchange for the rich sugary reward [which fungi receive from their association with trees], the fungi provide a few complimentary benefits for the tree, such as filtering out heavy metals, which are less detrimental to the fungi than to the tree's roots."[9] In keeping with the same compensatory system of exchange, fungi also support diverse species of trees underground, so that one species does not dominate to the exclusion of other species altogether.[10]

The effect of all such cases as just mentioned is not only an expanded view of hospitality but also what might call *communication by compensation*—or, in another lingo, by an implicit assessment of "exchange value." While occasionally there may be a direct message ("noxious insects are coming") that would be best conveyed in a biochemical language or another form of overt semiosis, often it is a matter of a state of alertness that Wohlleben prefers to designate as "information."[11] But what exactly is the status and working of such information? It is not reducible to sheer factuality; it is a matter of what Wohlleben calls "goods": nutrients and water. It is the passage of such goods that, short of any linguistic or semiotic medium, constitutes information: that is, these goods *inform* one system as to what is happening in another. The kind and level of the goods *is* the information and constitutes the crucial message that matters. All of this argues for a special form of attention in plants.[12]

If the precise *means* of communication vary, at least the *effect* is clear: "Social Security." These last two words form the title of a chapter in *The Hidden Life of Trees*, and they capture what is accomplished by the communicational network there under discussion. Social/Security: this signifies that the well-being of one member of a society is intimately connected with that of others, and they with it. No one member in a given society (for example, a beech tree in a grove of such trees) is fully secure unless certain entities subtending that society (the fungi in the soil that connects them) are also secure. As Wohlleben puts it, "a tree can be only as strong as the forest that surrounds it. . . . [Its] well-being depends on [its] community": a community that includes the fungi clustering at the base of the trees of that forest.[13] Even isolated trees remain connected, forming a nexus with other trees thanks to the fungal networks that extend far across open spaces: "a single fungus can cover many square miles and network an entire forest."[14]

Moreover, it has been established that the distribution of information through such a network is *equitably shared* among the trees it connects.[15] Here is an intimation of what one of us has called "vegetal communism."[16] The result is that "a tree can only be as strong as the forest that surrounds it."[17] This is not surprising if we consider that "it takes a forest to create a microclimate suitable for tree growth and sustenance."[18]

This extraordinary situation—little suspected by human beings, and all the less so in an era of modern individualism—is made even more extraordinary by a growing suspicion that something like *caring* occurs among the trees in a given forest. What for Heidegger had been the privilege of individuated human Dasein—its "care-structure"—is now actively imagined as inherent in the shared life of trees with each other. As Tim Flannery puts it: "the most astonishing thing about trees is how social they are. *The trees in a forest care for each other*, sometimes even going so far as to nourish the stump of a felled tree for centuries after it was cut down by feeding it sugars and other nutrients, and so keeping it alive."[19] Of course, the caring here posited is not meant to be the exact equivalent of human caring, but its arboreal analogue. Instead of its being directed exclusively onto another entity of the same species, here the cared-for other can be a member of an altogether different species of tree as in a mixed forest.

In this respect, the caring is quite radically democratic—where "democracy" signifies a coherent grouping of diverse individuals united by a resolution to determine their common destiny without giving up on their diversity. In the case of trees, there is no explicit resolution since there is no verbal language in which to formulate it; but there is nonetheless a united front of highly variegated individuals whose lot has been cast together even if not by anything like conscious choice. The sociality of trees extends deeply into arboreal life as it is lived in common among members of a given group of trees (a "forest," a "grove," a "patch" of trees).

Put otherwise, there is a clustering effect that suggests the spontaneous emergence of a distinctive sociality of trees-in-community that together form a *commons*. Such a commons is composed of highly diverse hospitalities—some not easily recognized as such—that are proffered between various members in radically different formats.

Community-as-*Commons*. We have seen that Sheldrake alludes to "community" in his discussion of fungal partnerships. The very word is richly suggestive, being formed from—*com* ("together," "with"—the Latin rendition of the Greek *sym* or *syn*) and *munity* from Greek *moin*, "held in common." Still more ancient is the Indo-European root *mei*, signifying "to go, move, change." A community, then, is a place where things come together—and in the case of living things like trees and fungi, where they *live together*: where they *live in common*, where they inhabit a *common space*, as occurs with the roots of trees and the soil in which they are embedded as well as the air with which they mingle and which they enrich with oxygen up above.

The "commons" is one such shared space, but it is usually construed as a space in which human beings have the major stake. In customary usage, a commons is "the undivided land belonging to the members of a local community as a whole."[20] But "members of a local community" could as well refer to trees, bacteria, fungi, and lichen as to human beings. In none of these cases is the commons transformed into property—not even collectively held property. It is shared without being objectified, and each member participates in, contributes to, and benefits from such a commons in a unique way. We are circling back to the sense of vegetal communism, alluded to earlier, via such a lived critique not only of the concept of private property as Marx and those who followed him offered but also of property *tout court*.

The residents of a commons become more resolutely human when the commons is considered a pact or contract, as in this formulation: "the commons is the contract a people make with their local natural system."[21] Plants and their fungal partners do not make formal contracts—which imply an entire legal system, language, and a certain regulated historicity. But we can imagine that there is something like an implicit contract between the denizens of a shared natural place: a tacit agreement, as it were, that does not require verbal expression. At stake here is something close to Gary Snyder's use of the term "Natural Contract": "We need to make a world-scale 'Natural Contract' with the oceans, the air, the birds in the sky. . . . Take back, like the night, that which is shared by us all, that which is our larger being . . . [our] direct involvement in sharing (in *being*) the web of the wild world."[22] Can we not think of trees—as well as a number of other plants—as forming a spontaneous natural contract with each other? Snyder affirms this when he writes that "the commons is a level of organization of human society that *includes the nonhuman*."[23] To be fair, we would need to invert the terms of inclusion if we are to account for the actual place of the human in the wider organic and inorganic realms. This would yield the following formulation: "the commons is a level of organization of nonhuman society that *includes the human*." Or, in the light of our current discussion, this can be amended further: "the commons is a level of organization that can happen among humans or among members of other species."

Key to this conception of the commons is what Snyder calls "*self-determination in place*,"[24] which is at the same time a co-determination of the places that coexist and codepend in a common space. Is this not just what we have been hearing from ecologists such as Sheldrake and Wohlleben—namely, that the communities of nonhuman beings (trees as well as other plants) they examine devise unique ways of determining their own ways of populating biocommons or biomes, which are their own self-generated spaces of shared coinhabitation?[25] Do not these modes of self-determination entail the equivalent of a contract among themselves: a tacit but deep commitment to meet their responsibilities as contributing members of a local community? Rousseau famously proposed a "natural contract" as at the origin of the state. Why not posit an even more deeply and fully *natural* contract between the denizens of the bioregions that trees and their entourage cocreate? "Showing solidarity with a region"[26]—is this not just what such an entourage exhibits in its most primal form? If for humans "the level above the local commons is the bioregion,"[27] then for trees the bioregion can be considered the level at which they exist; it is nothing other than the place where they interact in the innumerable ways that have been uncovered by ecologists in the last century and a half.

Part of belonging to a commons—whether human or other-than-human—is that the inhabitants *accompany* each other in a version of what Mary Watkins designates as "mutual accompaniment."[28] It is a matter of an especially intimate form of companionship in which the proximity of each member with all others is not merely a matter of spatial proximity—along with corresponding modes of temporal contiguity—but such that each member can be said to be essential to the well-being of all other members with which it coexists and interacts. What we earlier referred to as "care" for others can be seen as a feature of mutual accompaniment. This is not a matter of the ethics of caring, nor of the emotionality of caring, but rather a matter of a close attending to the other's presence and taking account of what this other (an other that is itself always multiple) is signaling to us by way of informative signs and alerting us to their distress. As the very word *accompany* signifies, it is a matter of keeping company with one's immediate companions: to be not merely present to them but to be *in their company* or, again, to be *at* their company: to be not merely with them but contiguous in several senses: close to them, receptive to them, welcoming to them. In short, a commons in this extended sense is a matter of mutual accompaniment, a situation of shared hospitality among all members, human and otherwise.

Watkins writes that "mutual accompaniment reverses the autoimmune response in our social bodies, building solidarity between realms, rather than division and self-destruction."[29] We can actively imagine that these words also apply to trees that coexist in a forest, or to a cluster of saplings at the edge of one's lawn, as well as to groupings of crops and plants. Each constitutes a natural commons, a closely knit community whose members accompany each other in a myriad of welcoming ways. This is a commons that comes to be in a given place—so much so that it constitutes the very being of that place: a place that is always already *in place* once it comes to exist as a common space for all the diverse forms of life it contains and supports.[30] If human beings are often concerned with what Watkins designates as a "commons-to-come"[31]— better forms of democracy and other forms of social and political coexistence—trees and their immediate surroundings constitute *commons-in-place*: commons already in place or coming to constitute a place they together share.

In the case of plants, such a common place is provided by the subtending soil and the atmosphere, and even the microclimates, with levels of humidity and oxygen dependent on vegetal communities. The porous character of such soil not only aerates it but facilitates the transmission of nutrients as well as urgent messages of warning and distress. Oele, in *E-Co-Affectivity*, argues that the dense interfaces of what is underground constitute a protosociety that can be taken as a model for a vision of human society as no longer based on competition between fiercely individuated human beings—as in the Anthropocene—but rather on modalities of subtle and ingenious interaction in what she designates as the "Soilocene": "Soil and its pores point the way and provide a living, connective tissue: beyond the concrete and discrete individual, here and now, refusing homogeneous space and standardized chronological time, they direct us toward other places, toward other times, toward solidarity with other beings, toward unexpected assemblages and gatherings."[32] Such soilocentric solidarity embodies a primal form of mutual hospitality. This interspecies hospitality is made possible in turn by the facticity of *shared place*. In the case of trees, as well as other plants, it is not a matter of *other* places and *other* times—of past places and places-to-come—but of *this very place*, the place where a welcoming accompaniment is now happening with the tacit heritage of past places and a bequeathal of future places, the soil and the atmosphere. This is the place that underlies and supports a given tree, but also groupings of proximally located trees that together constitute living communities in commons of mutual welcoming.

B. TREES IN PLACE

Our relation to the natural world takes place in a place.
Gary Snyder, *The Practice of the Wild*

You will have noticed how the language of "place" has emerged at several points in the foregoing discussion of the shared sociality of trees, suggesting that it is now time to address the *place of trees* more directly. It is altogether too humanocentric to presume that place is something that belongs to human beings alone—that humans exclusively create places, live in places, build in places, and remember places. One of us (EC) was drawn to writing on place as a result of his consideration of the *memory of place*: a neglected topic, yet one that presumes that remembering a place is something humans do—primarily if not exclusively.[33] But is this so?

We know that many nonhuman animals have *lairs*—home-places where they can seek security and safety. Bears return to their *dens*; birds have *nests* in which they raise entire families. These familiar examples indicate that place belongs to the cycle of *habitability on earth*. Its common trait is a certain durability. Were it to be merely momentary, it would not count as a place, which requires a *minimal stabilitas loci*—stable enough to count as somewhere to which return may be reliably made when rest is required or as protection from predators. Without such ongoing habitality, a place is no longer a place: it is merely a passing site.

All this is well known; but what about the place of trees—and of the fungal/bacterial/lichenid life forms associated with them? This is less often discussed and recognized. Here we need to distinguish between three modalities of emplacement: place of, place for, and place with.

Place of. The place of trees is their actual location: just where they are situated—say, in a given field or on the banks of a river or on an island in a river. This is a "where" that could be given cartographic specification, but to determine such a "where" on maps is the concern of human beings, not of trees themselves: the metrics of maps measure dimensions of the logistics that matter to owners of trees for various purposes (sale, beautification of property, management of a grove of trees, scientific measurement) but that do not matter to trees themselves: not *as such*, though locations in larger spaces can be considered part of the full actuality of the trees—a formal/numerical dimension, as it were, but not a dimension that is an integral part of the life of trees themselves or of their placiality.

The place of trees that matters for trees themselves—that is an integral part of their being-on-earth—we can call their *emplacement*. This is the discrete area where trees belong—not by predestination but because they have come to inhabit a given plot of land. *Plot*, a word that is etymologically linked both to *place* and to *plant*, signifies a discrete locus where something has come to take up residence—that is, to be situated there not just momentarily (as in a "place of passage") but in a comparatively lasting way: lasting sometimes for the life of the entity in question. A house that serves as a reliable dwelling place exists in a plot where its human residents can *return* reliably day after day, night after night. Trees, however, do not return; they *remain* where they are—to employ another *re* word that signifies staying-in-place rather than coming back to it. In short, *trees remain in place*—with notable exceptions, such as the already mentioned stilt palms that grow new exorrhiza, or external stiltlike roots (hence their name in scientific classification *Socratea exorrhiza*), which can move away from the original plot where they have grown in search of minerals and moisture in the soil by deactivating previous roots—but these exceptions do not disprove the overall arboreal norm of staying-in-place, of clinging to the place where they have been situated since their first flourishing as seeds in the soil of their origin.

It is this very feature of trees that endows them with what we often most admire about them: their abiding steadiness, their dignified upright bearing, their standing there before us, and (often but not always) towering over us. All these positive predicates stem from, and reflect, the place of trees, their uniquely arboreal emplacement, their being-in-place. This last locution, "being-in-place," can be taken as a concrete version of "being-in-the-world," Heidegger's phrase for the way that human Dasein engages the world it inhabits; but "world" in the Heideggerian sense includes culture and language—which are not in the repertoire of trees except by implication or mediated by biochemical, electrical, and other types of signals, as discussed earlier. Their *world* (if we are to use that term at all) is a world of bark, of leaves and branches, of roots, and, invisibly but potently, of fungal and bacterial presences that cluster in and through it, as well as the soil and solar energy. The place *of* a tree is a location for all this—and this is already a lot: a lot more than we can grasp at a glance.

Place for. The place of trees is a place for their flourishing—for their well-being: for their becoming what they can be within the limits of their genetic givens: their fore-plan, as it were. This fore-plan differs from one type of tree to another: from beech to chestnut, from oak to pine. The prospering of a given tree is not limitless; it happens within the schematic structure provided by the genetic basis of the tree type and, to a great extent, by its interaction with the unique features of the spot where it grows: the availability of sunlight and solar exposure, the composition of the soil and amounts of rainfall or underground water sources, and so forth. But within this structure considerable variation is possible. This is not "free variation" in Husserl's sense of the methodological variation of a given example or set of examples with the aim of getting at the abiding essence (*Wesen*) of a given type of thing. This is variation *within* a given type—in particular, within a type of tree such as, say, an elm—and of the *where of* its emplacement, as, say, in a mixed forest or in a backyard.

The place-for an elm is a place that aids and supports its free growth *as an elm*, as that kind of tree and no other. Such a sense of place includes all the ways it supports and, in many respects, steers such growth, actively contributing to its flourishing as that very elm we witness before us. Here one of us (EC) recalls the elm in the front yard of his boyhood home in Topeka, Kansas: tall, dignified, shading a significant part of the yard in summer, protecting it in winter snow. This single tree was a central presence in his entire childhood, and a recent visit to the same location in eastern Kansas revealed that the new owners had built a circular driveway around the elm as if to pay homage to its magisterial presence—now for a new family with their very different history. We can safely say that the front yard of my childhood home was, and remains, the *place for* this magisterial tree, whose arboreal magic continues in force over many decades thanks to its being in a place propitious for its support and sustenance. We assert this without having to "prove" it by biochemical analysis of the constituents of that place: its root system, its subsoil, or even the characteristic (and doubtless changing) climate of that particular location east of the Flint Hills in Kansas. Not that such scientific analysis is without interest; it holds its own fascination; but it is not required for us to appreciate that this particular elm, in all its uniqueness, has done well in the very place where it is to be found in a particular locus in Topeka. It has prospered despite the onset of the Dutch Elm disease that devastated many trees of the same species further east in the United States during the 1950s. It survived this lethal threat, and doubtless many other unrecorded challenges, to become what it is: a stately tree with its own identity and its own bearing: its own *being*.

This being is a being-in-place that is the right place for it to be or (considered retrospectively) to have been and, hopefully, still to be in the future. This is not to say that it is the only place where it could have done so well. The place-for is not necessarily unique. It can be realized in multiple locations and widely various climatic conditions. But in the case of the elm here described, the tree at 3210 W. 17th St., the place-for was just right—right enough anyway for it to assume the commanding presence by which it figured in one of this book's author's lifetime and now for other residents of the same residential lot in Topeka, Kansas.[34]

Place-for thus proffers a *forward edge* to the place of trees. Beyond sheer location considered as place-of, this dimension of place underlines all the ways—too many to detail here—in which place contributes constructively to the life of trees while trees communally and symbiotically contribute to the life of places. It provides not just a minimal material basis for this twofold life (via the tree's exposure to air and light and its root system) but offers opportunities for growth and enhancement that would not be available in a less propitious place.

The life of a tree is thus doubly dependent on its particular emplacement: dependent on there being a place at all for it to be what it is and where it is, but also dependent on there being a place that actively contributes to its well-being, to what we cannot help but call its "flourishing"—which means not just its surviving but its *doing well* in terms of the unique criteria that obtain for a given species of tree: becoming a stronger and more lasting and more diversely differentiated tree than would be the case if such a place-for were lacking.

Place-with. The sociality of trees reaches a certain climax in terms of their comparative *withness:* their being-together-with in various senses. *Being-with their own immediate ambience* is the trees' being-with the soil in which they are rooted as well as the fungal mass that underlies them and that permeates this same soil; this is in effect a being-with-itself, since these underlying factors form part of a tree's own complete and complex identity. This is analogous to the way in which human beings are with-their-own-body, a state that Merleau-Ponty calls "the lived body" whereby I sense that I am at one with myself—with my corporeal self, with the body that subtends, supports, and animates my ongoing daily life. As Sheldrake puts it, "Our bodies, like those of all other organisms, are dwelling places."[35] I am my lived body, which is my ongoing dwelling place so long as I am alive. My body is the place that is most intimately *mine*—where I am most fully myself—and yet it is also a habitat in its own right, a place for other forms of life, such as gut bacteria that make the digestive and, therefore, nourishing processes possible.

Much the same can be said for the soil and root system of a tree. The tree *is* them by being so intimately *with* them as to be inseparable from them as its place-to-be: destroy them and you destroy the tree that towers above them, just as to destroy the basic viability of my lived body is to destroy the very basis of my being-in-the-world, my existing there. It is a matter, minimally, of the tree and its rootedness *being-with each other in the same place*: a place that enables them to be with one another.

Above the ground, we encounter the sociality of trees in the most manifest manner, their being together with one another in full sight: that is, being together as a coherent cluster of trees, a *copse* or a *grove* in earlier English nomenclature. The fact that each tree in this cluster has its own unique history does not prevent it from congregating with other proximal trees in a unique kind of gathering. Individual trees are with each other by being alongside each other; but putting it this way overlooks the intimacy of their shared space and their sensitivity to one another. Often enough, trees that appear to be separate aboveground share the rooting system below ground level. Instead of words, they exchange biochemical substances and subtle movements. The branches of one tree reach out to those of the tree next to it yet seem to be careful not to touch these other branches. The leaves of a given tree appear to move in rhythm with those of its partners thanks to a local wind that caresses them both and unites them, however briefly. They can be said to exhibit *interbeing*: their interaction allows them to exist together as one complex but coherent cluster. It follows that for such groupings of trees " 'to be' is to inter-be."[36]

Such inter-being is not spoken, but it is occasionally *seen*, and we humans and other animals can witness it from where we stand, near or far as this may happen to be. This means that we as witnesses are swept up into this same sociality: members-at-the-edge quite literally, members-at-large more generally. But the main event is the socializing of the trees themselves, their being-with one another, their existing in proximity to each other as in a space of intimate contiguity. Even if they do not touch, they are within touching distance—a distance determined by the being of trees themselves, bridged in springtime by pollinating insects who convey parts of genetic material from one blossoming tree to another and varying from species to species and even by the comparative ages of the trees that socialize in the distinctive ways to which we have pointed earlier. And in still other subtle ways: so many, indeed all too many, to document here in any detail, but ways that tree lovers and tree watchers know well.

Taken together, all these modalities of being-with each other constitute a crucial dimension of what Richard Powers designates as "The Overstory."[37] In his extraordinary novel bearing this title, Powers shows how trees stand *over* human lives, connecting them and protecting them—say, a single chestnut tree on a farm in western Iowa that, in its sheer survival, linked several generations of the Hoel family, which first settled there in the mid-nineteenth century. This one tree goes it alone after nearby trees vanish under the soil: arboreal sociality is here condensed into this single remaining tree, which "bulks out. Its bark spirals upward like Trajan's Column. Its scalloped leaves carry on turning sunlight into tissue. It more than abides; it flourishes, a globe of green health and vigor."[38] This health and vigor sustain the Hoel family through at least six generations as well as inducing neighbors to admire it and take inspiration from it: it comes to be known to locals as the "sentinel tree." Thus, even if a strictly arboreal collegiality of several proximal trees has vanished, a single remaining chestnut exudes a longitudinal social space that gathers around it not only members of the Hoel family over generations but admiring neighbors as well. Thus is the place-with of this extraordinary tree shown to include human beings as well as the underground world that acts to sustain it for centuries in all the varying weather conditions that obtain in Iowa. Its place-with is a place shared with others—human and nonhuman alike. The sociality of trees, even if not directly realized in the case of a solitary tree, extends outward to include human (and likely other animal) admiring witnesses.

None of this would be possible were it not for the way that continuity of place underlies the entire history of a given tree, just as it subtends entire groves of trees such as one sometimes sees at the edges of farmland in the American South. Such placial continuity makes possible not only the literal life of such trees, but it gives to them a coherence they would otherwise lack. Being the place-of a single tree or group of trees, it is a place-for their conjoint prospering (and sometimes for their common perishing, as when diseases pass from tree to tree) as well as a place-with: a place that enables them to be with one another and with other life-forms (from fungal and bacterial to insectile and human) in coherent and lasting ways.

The sociality of trees is an important constituent feature of ecology overall. Such sociality supports the view that ecology is all about the coexistence of diverse organisms—sometimes of these organisms with others of the same kind, sometimes with living entities of another kind, and often both at once. Yet, given an undeniable fascination with the details of the lives of individual organisms, including how they cooperate in a case of a given kind as well as their living arrangements with other kinds, we tend to overlook their distinctive emplacements.

The scale at which such emplacement happens is much more extensive than we usually assume. We normalize it as occurring at a scale that befits our own all too human scale. But emplacements abound at every level of life on earth, even at the microbial, as Sheldrake describes it: "Horizontal gene transfer transformed bacterial genomes into cosmopolitan places; endosymbiosis transformed cells into cosmopolitan places.... Upon arrival in a new place, the fungus must meet a compatible photobiont and form their relationship afresh."[39] Note the ease with which this statement recurs to "place" and "places" in the very midst of describing a quite complex ecological concept that bears on something as microscopic as genes.

We affirm that place, rather than being something merely adventitious—a matter of just where something happens to be located—is essential to ecology construed in its original sense:

"The word *ecology* has its roots in the Greek word *oikos* meaning 'house,' 'household,' or 'dwelling *place*.'"[40] Of these three optional etymological roots of *ecology*, we take "dwelling place" to be the most important for our purposes. Houses and households belong properly to the human species and thus to other species only by metaphorical extension. But the emplacement of trees involves their own dwelling places, given that trees take up residence in very particular places that support them physically and nurture them nutritionally. An ecology of trees must include serious consideration of their dwelling places: places where they not only exist but flourish and eventually die.

We have just seen that arboreal emplacement assumes three distinctive forms: place-of, place-for, and place-with. Our focus has been on how these three modalities of place obtain for trees even as we must also acknowledge that they obtain for other living species as well, however differently in given cases. But trees we take to be cardinal examples of the ecology of emplacement, thanks to their ongoing and overbearing presence in our lives on earth. They are exemplary cases of a naturally given commons—a commons that we find with us, around us, under us, and over us in our time on earth. Trees are our most steady nonhuman living partners, and we count on them for much more than many of us consciously realize. They are the ongoing overstory of our lives and are to be treasured as such, alongside the recognition of the value of arboreal flourishing in its own right.

What Michael Perlman calls "the power of trees" consists very much in their being gifted with multiple modes of emplacement.[41] Whereas human beings tend to specialize in their dedication to finding or constructing secure modes of dwelling places—"home is where the heart is," as we say glibly and all too revealingly, as if to justify our obsession with comfort and mutual support—trees exhibit a genius for diverse ways of being in and with their own places and thus for our being with them in places we ourselves could never construct, nor live in full-time. Trees take us to radically other, nonhuman places—without which, however, human places would be unviable. They take us *elsewhere*, away from the protection of walls and the history of houses, affording another kind of protection and another sort of history: *their* protection and *their* history. In their very difference from what we know in our own highly domesticated lives, they exemplify what exposure to the unharnessed elements, to all kinds of weather, to predation, and to radically different destinies is like. They draw us out as well as keep us in—*out* into their inspiring but sometimes threatening embrace and *in* to the protection they can offer in a major storm. In this dialectic of drawing out and keeping in, they exhibit the singular genius of their extra-ordinary powers of emplacement.

Interlude 3

PLANTS FROM AFAR

As Seen in Landscape Painting

Until now, we have been discussing plants as we directly experience them in perceiving them and in otherwise interacting with them. But they are also present to us indirectly in photography and cinema and in paintings. Leaving aside their photographic and cinematic presence for a separate study,[1] we shall restrict ourselves here to discussing various ways in which plants are conveyed to us in paintings.

We start with a paradox, very much in line with the paradoxes that have accompanied us all along in this study: how can the *places* of plants be given painterly representation if it is the case (as we have argued earlier) that such places, though entirely real and indeed necessary to the life of plants and of entire ecosystems they sustain, are nevertheless indeterminate, evading exact measurement? In a word valorized by Charles Sanders Peirce, the presence of such places is intrinsically *vague*. The further paradox is that it is precisely this character of places that makes them prime candidates for being painted. Were they to be altogether determinate, they would call for different modes of representation: namely, cartographic or photographic rather than painterly. In that case, pictorial exactitude would be in order. Although there is certainly such a thing as "realist" painting, even here the aim is not to produce a reliable and precise depiction as such but to offer the image of something whose physical analogue may be exact in measurement—say, a plate in its very rotundity—but now rendered in terms of its qualitative presence in lines and colors. This requires considerable artistic skill rather than scientific acumen or photographic finesse.

With painting, we move from the discursive treatments we have given to plants—treatments offered in philosophical and scientific language—to a medium that is decisively nonverbal and, in this very regard, very well suited to convey the expressiveness of vegetal life itself. Nevertheless, we shall discuss this painterly medium by means of words in order to convey our understanding of what painting accomplishes. The result will be a hybrid text, employing bivalent expressive means by way of moving back and forth between image and word.

"Image" we take to refer to something mainly pictorial—a depiction, that is, taking an image (qua "*pict*-ure") *from* (via the *de-* in de-piction) something that both in itself and for itself is nonpictorial: say, a flower, bush, or tree. This image need not be of something easily named as such. But it must convey to us a sense of something we can encounter in an open sensory field: where "open" includes whatever is accessible in vision or direct touch or smell. It can also encompass items in the very different field of *mental* vision, including things and events that we remember or imagine. But our concern here is with the painting of things that are objects of direct sight and touch and smell and that belong to the natural world: namely, plants. These objects need not be realistically rendered—though an element of recognizability, however indirect or even abstract, inheres in what we experience in viewing a painting of them.

I

One of us (EC) recalls that among the first paintings he ever did—as part of a class in watercolor for young people at a local art museum—was a depiction of a large elm tree on the college campus where the same museum was located. He remembers being drawn to this particular tree (since then destroyed in a tornado that hit the campus in 1966) as if to something awesome and even numinous. He felt he had to paint *it*, that one enormous tree with its widely outspread limbs and branches, being drawn to it as if to an enormous magnet. He sat under this gigantic living being, painting its image on a large sheet of paper stationed on a plywood board.

Here we must ask: What was happening here? I was certainly not trying to paint a "realist" picture. I was already, at age eight, aware that I could never match a photograph in terms of detailed depiction—and didn't want to try to do so. Instead, I was attempting to capture the *experience* of being under the all-embracing presence of that tree to which I was so powerfully drawn. In the image I created, the tree was there not as a discrete object on a college lawn but as the central force in a field of forces; it was a dynamic event at the heart of an experiential field. It had a being—and a becoming—of its own; but this was only as part of a larger whole that included bushes and other trees in that corner of the campus. And it included myself; though not depicted as such, my being-there was inseparable from the way this painting, in all its awkwardness and naivete, captured the moment. And it was part of that moment itself; the painting and what was painted, along with all that surrounded them— all this was swept up into this same multidimensional event.

This event itself was singular in at least two respects. First, it occurred at a moment that was never to be repeated (though it can certainly be remembered, as I am now doing). If that moment condensed the singular temporality of this occasion, the tree itself was the singular spatial presence, given its dominance in my painting and in the original scene itself. But a tree such as the elm is not just any object. It is a living being that towers overhead and spreads out laterally and is also attached to the earth at its base. Although I did not depict this base in the painting, it was a felt presence: the elm would not have been what it was without its underlying presence. I was no burgeoning botanist but an aspiring artist; yet I could not overlook the rootedness of the tree in the soil of the land on which I sat to paint: it was an integral part of the situation in which I was painting that particular tree. I was *close to this rootedness*—so close that I did not discern it as anything discrete but took it for granted without knowing anything specifically about its importance for the tree and the surrounding land. This not-knowing-in-detail is an integral part of most of our being up close to plants, being part of their circumambience.

At stake here was also *place*—which had its own indeterminate presence in such a scene. In the moment I am here recalling, I was undisputedly *at the place* of the tree. As we have argued, the place of plants does not yield to direct determination, if this means measurability in standard units of feet, inches, or meters. Despite this indefiniteness of extent, it serves as the *place of* and *place for* whatever living plant is located there where it stands and is rooted in the soil. No wonder I did not try to represent it as such in my fledgling painting. I was *in it*—so much so that it was my place as well as the tree's: we both belonged to the same extended place whose primary occupant was the tree that dominated both my experience and my painting. I was so intimately *on it*—this very place—that I was *in it*, part of it: so much so that it would have been very difficult to give it separate representation. Painting place is a special challenge at any point, but all the more so if it is the place in which the painter is himself located. This says something important about the place of plants, including trees: such place resists recognizable representation, so much so that it rarely appears as such in a painting, including a painting of individual plants. And this is so even though we know that plants certainly have their places on earth and inhabit them: how else could they *be there*? Where else could they be?

Such resistance to the discrete representation of place is an important but rarely recognized characteristic of efforts to represent arboreal and herbaceous presence. We have just seen that it is an intrinsic feature of close-up views of such presence. But what is place as seen *from afar*, as it figures into painting scenes from the natural world?

II

Directionally regarded, a painting such as the early effort I have described emphasizes the UP and OUT, as viewed from DOWN and UNDER. These directional adverbs indicate vectors characterizing views of something that is seen. Precisely as a view—albeit one seen from a position in proximity to the represented thing (here a giant elm tree), it lacks the immediacy of touch—as when touching moss, in the example examined in the second interlude. It is still the depiction of something seen from a certain distance, diminutive as this may be when the person painting is stationed right under the tree that is the main figure of the painting.

What then about paintings of plants, such as trees, as shown at greater distances? Here we enter the domain of *landscape painting.* By its etymology, *landscape* signifies *shape of the land*—thus of parts of the earth as seen from afar and no longer from up close: seen from far enough away to take on a visible contour such as the horizon or the underlying earth given as a single stretch. At play here is the presentation of earth—and of what resides on earth—from a certain distance: a distance that cannot be measured in so many determinate units but that can no longer be considered as close up. This is a presented distance that is sufficient to offer a certain *spectacle* of things presented in the painting as set on earth.

Take, for example, this painting by Claude Monet:

Figure int3.1. Monet, *Banks of the Seine, Vétheuil*, 1880. Chester Dale Collection at the National Gallery of Art. Reproduced on p. 495 in John Walker, *National Gallery of Art* (New York: Abrams), p. 494.

Here we have a painting of both nonarboreal plants (the dense bushes in the foreground) and trees (in the background: at and as the horizon) with a river in between. Among several outstanding features we note these:

> the downward thrust of the bushes, anchoring them in the underlying but not visible ground;
> the sheer verticality of the distant trees, which seem to move UP and DOWN at once: up into the sky, down into the earth on the far bank of the Seine;
> an adumbration of *emplacement* at both the bush and tree levels: for the bushes, a scattered but distinctly subjacent grounding, supportive of the numerous plants from underneath even if not shown as such; this is in contrast with a distinct sense of secure placement in the case of the trees in the distance; these seem decisively *set on earth*, one by one, and to grow right out of it up into the sky, even as we imagine their roots to sink down deep into the earth, this descent being reinforced by the dark reflections of the trees in the water that connect upper and lower parts of the same painting.

All this is shown thanks to the view being long-range—long enough to allow for a complex but coherent combination of features, each of which is seen from a certain felt but not precisely measurable distance. This distance allows for the items represented in the painting to be shown standing alone: if not altogether apart, then as distinctively situated in relation to each other. But it also allows for the conjunction of all these features, as if seen in a single sweeping glance—a glance originally Monet's but bequeathed to us as latter-day viewers of this accomplished work. Its middle-range physical size (28 7/8" x 39 3/8") allows the painting to encompass all this complexity without crowding it, to lend it an expansiveness that is the pictorial analogue of a single human glance at the environing landscape—seeing just this much, but not more. A landscape painting, no matter how expansive it may be, cuts off the view at some decisive point, whereas a look at an actually perceived landscape is indefinitely extendable with a mere turning of the viewer's head. In the latter case, the affordances (in J. J. Gibson's term) are in principle unlimited, whereas a landscape painting offers us a determinate set of affordances—those allowed by what is included in the presented pictoriality of the painted scene. Whereas Monet himself could look up and down the Seine at Vétheuil freely and without inhibition, we can only look—and see—as far as his painting allows.

Despite their inherent restrictions on the scope of what they present, landscape paintings give us entire worlds composed of earth and water, plants and sometimes animals—all in a single coherent commixture. Paintings done close up, as with my childhood rendition of a towering elm, offer restricted parts only of full landscapes by focusing on a certain distinct member of the larger landscape. This larger layout is not given in the presented image but can be inferred to reside around the focal features that are singled out in the close-up view. In such cases, we are given finite parts of a landscape, elements of a larger world but not this world itself. There is an undeniable and often attractive intimacy in such close-up paintings, which allow us to appreciate a single bush or tree or a cluster of either. But we lack the larger and more generous view that a more replete landscape affords—so large and generous in certain cases that it amounts to the presentation of the *sublime* in Kant's sense of what inspires in us an appreciation whose scope and affective tenor are akin to the undelimited deployment of pure reason when it asserts its full power of knowing.[2]

III

When we are in the lived presence of an open landscape, we sense ourselves immersed in it, an integral part of it even if we are viewing it from a particular vantage point. This vantage point is often experienced as an edge of the scene we behold—an edge that belongs at once to the scene itself and to ourselves. It is a viewing point aiming outward toward a landscape as well as a stance taken up by our own lived body—both at once. This situation differs decisively from the experience of looking at a painting of the same landscape. In this case, we feel ourselves to be decisively *outside* the landscape itself, external to it and viewing it via its represented image.

We are not looking into a landscape of which we are already an integral (if literally peripheral) part but a landscape that is in a space of its own—that is entirely contained in the painted image itself, framed by it, as it were. Moreover, we can reach out and touch that image directly, whereas in the direct perception of an actual landscape we can point to various features of it but we cannot touch it, the landscape itself. Touchable in its finite parts, the actual landscape is untouchable as a whole. It is what we above called a "spectacle"—all there to be seen but not to be touched as such.

Moreover, there is something self-contained about a landscape painting that is not the case with regard to a directly experienced landscape. Such self-seclusion distinguishes a landscape painting from a directly perceived landscape, one in which we are bodily immersed and as such *part of it*. The painting can be altogether "accurate" in terms of presenting detailed features of a landscape—including its plants—and yet even the most meticulous and "realistic" painting does not take us *there*: out there in anything comparable to what we experience when we actively enter the landscape scene itself. We view the painting *from a different place*—say, in an art gallery or our living room—compared to where we are when we are included in the landscape scene itself. This is the difference between touching a tree while seated under it and producing a painting of this same tree—a tree that, as painted, we cannot reach out to and feel with our hand. This untouchable tree has become viewable only in a format that presents its image: it has come to exist in this phantom presence, which reaffirms the vegetal subjectivity of the tree itself. Attractive as this image may be, it exists at a distance we cannot span with our lived body: not because it is too far away but because its mode of being, represented rather than perceived, is inherently untraversable. Just as a nonphysical distance between two subjectivities, whether human or not, is ultimately irreducible.

IV

Given this basic difference between a painted and a directly experienced landscape, what does it portend for the representation of plants? Here we reach another paradox: precisely as represented, plants or trees can be thematized in paintings in ways that infrequently happen when they are perceived as belonging to a directly experienced landscape. In that case, they are unlikely to be thematized and will tend to fade "into the background," where they figure as secondary presences, if they are noticed at all: for example, as we move along on a walk in the woods guided by a concerted forward look so as not to lose our way. Our experiencing is then primarily taken up with the whole view—the scene given to us *all at once*. In this circumstance, we find ourselves invested in the full prospect before us and only rarely in its constituents taken separately. When a tree suddenly captures our full attention, it is exceptional and we know it to be such. Whereas we are not at all surprised when a painting singles out certain features rather than others: such as those of the particular bushes and trees that are made manifest in Monet's *Banks of the Seine, Vétheuil*. Paintings of plants are inherently, and highly, selective.

Monet had to chose what to include in his painting and what to exclude. Such definitive choice-making contrasts with a person actually perceiving the Seine at that particular point while walking beside it at the same historical moment when Monet was painting it. This walker is inundated with a myriad items, only some of which ended up in Monet's highly selective work. It is thanks to this very selectivity that landscape painting is well suited to bring to our collective attention components of full landscapes that we are likely to ignore when in the midst of traversing these same landscapes without the selectivity the painter exercises. These components include the very plants that only rarely stand out when walking through the same landscape that contains them. We pass through or by them without singling them out—without focusing on them as we would do if we were painting the same landscape scene. Even if we are suddenly struck by a certain bush or tree, we are unlikely to pause long enough to scrutinize it up close unless we are botanists—or landscape painters.

Landscape painting takes us out of direct engulfment in the plant world—an engulfment we experience every time we are out taking a stroll beyond city limits. As our earlier treatment of walking among plants made clear, this is a *per*ambulation—a "walking *through*" whatever the natural world provides, even if this is sometimes shaped by walking paths that we are inclined to follow. In perambulating in nature, we are moving largely on its terms rather than our own. We are *there in it*, part of it at least momentarily, and it is part of us as well: we *take it in* as we move through it.

All this changes radically when the same land we were traversing while walking is painted. Now we experience it at arm's length—the length of a landscape painter's arm as she transfigures the surrounding landscape into a *landscape painting*. Suddenly we experience a landscape in and by the medium of paint as it attaches to paper or canvas. We experience it in the painter's terms: in accordance with her vision, which shapes what she wishes to include or pass over, to emphasize or underplay, while conveying something of the place and the subjectivity of the plants inhabiting it

Here the latitude of her vision—assuming she is painting in front of an actual landscape, or at least remembering that landscape in some specific way (by sketches, her own internal memory, or perhaps with reference to comparable landscape paintings by artists she admires), or else imagining it actively without reference to any prior experience of it—joins forces with what she actually chooses to create: namely, *this* rendition of a real or remembered or imagined landscape that has inspired her to represent it in *just this way* . . . The fixity of the final image is not a liability but provides a mode of access for viewers of the painting who can scrutinize it carefully, return to it, remember its specificity in its physical absence. The viewer may not be able to walk among the plants depicted in a given painting, but the consolidation of the final image allows this viewer to return to the *same* painting time and again. Thanks to such returnability, what might seem like a constriction of experience brings its own expansive virtues, given that the viewer will see different aspects of the same painting on different viewings. (And, in certain cases, landscape painters themselves return to the same place to render it in paintings with seasonal variations or at distinct times of the day, with differing natural lighting effects. Notable in this respect are the artists associated with the Group of Seven in Canada, who depicted the same landscapes in Northern Ontario at regular periods throughout a year.)

A landscape painting takes its viewer *there*—there to an actual, remembered, or imagined scene. Despite its status as a representation, it is an entity in its own right: with its own allure, its own magic. The fact that it is not the equivalent of an actual experience of a literal landscape does not undermine its power to attract us to it. We may never have viewed the Seine at Vétheuil, yet Monet's painting of it gives us the poignant pictorial equivalent of a scene that Monet himself experienced in first person (as we know from his usual practice of painting, or at least sketching, in plein air, even if finishing the painting in his studio). Confronting this art work, we are taken into its ambience by means of its selective format. Its scenic virtues draw us in—not to a full-scale world such as we might experience if we were present in person at that very place on the Seine, but to its iconic condensation by way of the painter's knowing selection of certain features of it. These features prominently include bushes and trees as well as a river; we are ushered into their pictorial compresence, being invited to accept the implicit hospitality of the painting as we contemplate it in admiration and gratitude. The fact that we are treated to views of bushes and trees and river at a certain pictorial distance does not lessen the gentle force of their appearing before us in a painted image rather than in the reality of witnessing them *in propria persona*. Such distance itself allows them to coinhere in the scene we are offered by the artist, thereby lending them a special allure and charm that only a painting of them can offer. We are ushered into their pictorial presence and given a mediated but vital insight into their living reality.

Three final remarks are in order:

1. Landscape paintings draw attention to the otherwise inconspicuous, backgrounded presence of plants. In such paintings, the woods, the fields, and so forth, are not a set of stage decorations for the main action to be enacted by humans or other animals; rather, these natural beings become the main *subjects* both in the colloquial and in the more restricted sense of the word. In Monet's painting, it is the tall trees in the distance, the bushes in the foreground, and the river between them that are the primary actors on this scene, where they play themselves out in a graceful coperformance.

2. We can say that in many landscape paintings what is often treated as the background moves to the foreground, without necessarily becoming a dominant figure: as with the trees in Monet's painting. This process, however incomplete it may be in a given case, is one of emergence or transition from the background to the foreground. Landscape painters know how to facilitate this emergence with dexterity; Monet did it with genuine genius.

3. Finally, artists and viewers alike share in the placiality of whatever is presented in a landscape painting. The painter brings the viewer, at least momentarily and pictorially, *into the place of plants*—however elusive this place itself may be. If so, this constitutes a special kind of reunion between otherwise radically disparate things: a form of visual magic that is uniquely performed by a landscape painting such as *Banks of the Seine, Vétheuil*.

5

ATTACHMENT AND DETACHMENT IN THE PLACE OF PLANTS

A. ATTACHMENT

I

Not only are we attracted to particular plants, but we can become attached to them, seeking them out at every opportunity, photographing or painting them, displaying them prominently in our homes, giving them to others as gifts. These are all ways of *doting on plants*, and there are many other such ways as well. But we only rarely feel a comparable regard for the *places* of plants: where they are situated and sustained. Such places are often barely noticed when we are in the presence of plants themselves: for the most part, we take such places for granted. If plants are often relegated to a green backdrop for whatever happens in a phenomenon sometimes referred to as "plant blindness," then the places of plants are doubly backgrounded and overlooked. When we describe a plant we love or admire to a friend, we concentrate on its upper, visible parts—the flowers, the leaves, the branches. But we are unlikely to focus on the place in which the plant we admire is itself situated or even to mention its subterranean parts. We assume it is there, but we are not inclined to look into it further, much less to take it seriously. It has a *sub rosa* presence rather than being something singular or distinct and worth attending to in its own right.

And yet, as we have been arguing, the place of plants is entirely essential to their existence and well-being. No plant can do without it, even if we are ill prepared to say just what it is and just how it is crucial to the life of any and all plants. Without exception, plants have distinctive places, however dimly we may be aware of them, much less affirm them with confidence. Even as plants are attached to particular places—*their own places*—we pay little attention to these places if we notice them at all. How can this be?

Every plant is emplaced. It could not be the living entity it is without such emplacement. Thanks to their root systems, plants are firmly attached to the particular places on which they depend for their well-being. Yet, however much we admire given plants, we rarely attend to their emplacement as such. Plants (including trees) are always located in a particular place, and yet this place is notably elusive when it comes to its description and its role in the lives of humans, who (with the exception of gardeners and dedicated amateurs) are notably unappreciative of its presence. This is so even if such presence is essential to the life of the very plants to which we are powerfully drawn and thus to our own existence as beings who live in their midst and depend on them for our very survival.

Bluntly put: whatever our own personal attachment to plants, we overlook their own attachment to the soil and earth in which they are deeply situated. How are we to understand such systematic neglect?

One reason for the neglect is the oculocentric assumption that if something exists, it must be visible. But this is certainly not the case, as we know from a range of phenomena that extends from crystals in rocks to brains in skulls—none of which is directly visible, yet all of which we know to exist. The same is true of significant parts of the place of plants. The parts of a plant that are underground may not be visible when the plant is seen from above, yet they are essential to the life of that same plant and to its having its own place on earth.

More generally, a place need not be visible in order to be a place. Some aspects of places are indeed visible, but this is a secondary characteristic, since many places are present yet not seen as such. In the case of plants, place is an underlying element, and, as a significant part of it is underground, it is not visible in its entirety. We sense its presence *down there*—somehow, somewhere under the visible parts of the plant whose place it is. Integral to its being the place of a plant is precisely its *not* being altogether visible.

At the same time, there may well be parts of a plant's place that *are* visible. We refer to the topsoil of the ground in which a given plant is located. This is, as it were, the *upper surface* of the place of the plant: where it emerges into sight and light, where it comes forward into view at and as the basis of a plant, the arena on which it stands and from which it expands upward and outward as *this* plant, the plant I now behold if I pause before it or that I may notice as I am passing by. Such a place is at once visible and invisible, both at once and indefeasibly so. Being above and below ground, it is an essentially hybrid factor, possessing a twofold existence that nevertheless constitutes one single place: *the place of this plant*.

This place is as extraordinary as it is ordinary. Ordinary as at least in part visible; extraordinary as *both* visible and invisible. It is when we emphasize its invisibility—its underground existence— that we tend to overlook the place of plants altogether. We bypass its existence out of ontological uneasiness at having to deal with something having such a directly contrary set of characteristics: better to move on than to have to deal with such a bivalent situation. No wonder we so often overlook the place of plants, given its uneasy commixture of visible and invisible dimensions.

II

The situation is further complicated when we try to assess the factor of *attachment*. We are not here speaking of attachment as a form of affection or liking for particular plants but of the facticity of plants as attached or connected to the places in which they exist—or better, where they *in-sist* ("sit in"). For *plants are attached to the earth*. They are bound to earth in ways that humans and other mobile beings are not. And they are attached to earth in and through the places where they reside. This is the very basis of their sessility, as we discuss it in chapter 1: their lack of intentional mobility understood as locomotion. (If they are mobile, it is due to their becoming uprooted or, as in the case of tumbleweeds, not stably rooted in the first place.)

Thinking along these lines, we obtain the following trilevel model:

1. Plants as visible living things: "aboveground"
2. Their places as bases of attachment to the earth
3. The earth taken as what underlies plants and their places alike

The places of plants are thus the indispensable *tertium quid* between the aboveground parts of plants (the visible parts: stem, branches, leaves, flowers) and the underground (roots, etc.). In this respect, such places serve to *mediate* between the aboveground aspects of plants and what is underground.

The bare fact that the earth level is not visible does not mean that it is any less potent; on the contrary, research has shown that roots inhabiting this level are quite arguably the most dynamic parts of plants. For roots are *roots in the earth*—a very deep mode of attachment. It is a matter of what Husserl came to call the "earth-basis" (*Erdebode*) of all life on this planet, thereby privileging this one of the ancient elements over the others (fire, air, water). If plants require air and water and sunlight to live and flourish, they are still more deeply dependent on the earth as their ultimate home-place.

It follows that *the ultimate and deepest attachment of plants is to the earth*. Here we are construing *earth* in its twofold significance: locally, as the container of soil, that into which the roots of plants reach as into their home-base; cosmically, as one of the ancient but still contemporaneously pertinent "elements" regarded as ultimate factors of the world as experienced by animals and plants alike.

The comparative innocence and simplicity of plants as we encounter them, one at a time or in groups, conceals a much deeper dimension: their role as paradigmatic attachments of life on earth. Where other living beings proceed more by detachment in their sheer mobility, plants embody and exemplify attachment itself. They manifest what it is to be *directly attached to the earth*; they depend on such attachments as inseparable from their well-being. Moreover, such earth-bound attachment occurs in and by means of the places where they are situated on earth itself—where "place" is at once the immediate plot of land in which a given plant is located *and* the means by which connection with the earth occurs below this plot. Every such place— every place of every plant—is an *earth-place*, a form of place we need to recognize as unique in its constitution and operation, considering it as providing the subtext for the life of plants and, by extension, as exemplary for all life on earth, including human life.

The attachment of plants through their places runs deep—extending profoundly into the earth as subtending everything that lives as well as what is nonliving. In this respect, plants lead the way for life on earth (as manifested in their being the forerunners of other kinds of complex life). They *bring us down to earth* by exemplifying, indeed *being*, paradigmatic modes of deep attachment to earth.

III

The attachment of plants goes two major ways—deep and wide. So far, we have concentrated on a primarily downward directionality in such attachment, focusing as we have on the way plants attach to their place and to the earth below: moving down twice. But plants also move upward. Often, we assume that higher on a vertical scale is better. But here we encounter a two-way situation: with plants, the upper level of the visible plant is not necessarily more valuable than that of the roots; in fact, the latter are arguably more essential to the life of plants—to their "intelligence."[1] Here we have a very different situation than that of the hierarchy of values in ancient Greek culture, whereby a higher location in a given hierarchy brings with it an increased value, as we see with Platonic Ideas vs. the entities or events in which these Ideas are instantiated. With plants, we have something like the reverse: not only are the roots of very special importance and value, but the underlying earth is arguably of supreme value, as we have come to appreciate in an era of increased environmental awareness such as our own.[2]

Some plants spread outward, efflorescing on their sides, as if reaching out in and from their place on the ground. Their perceived directionality is largely *horizontal*, as if they are reaching out to embrace the latitude of their lived place. Such sidewise directionality is at once a reaching out and a taking in: reaching out toward the immediate environs of their emplacement as defined by its outer edges and taking in what it has to offer in a gesture of receptivity. Instead of being part of a vertical hierarchy of values, this dimension of plants exhibits a spirit of receptivity, taking in with an open embrace what the surroundings have to offer—even if we know that plants can also be highly selective in what they come to accept or reject. The result of such horizontal outreach is a dialectic of acceptance and rejection that has everything to do with a plant's health in regard to the amounts of sunlight or rain, the effects of pollinating or herbivorous insects, and so forth. Underground, there is a subterranean analogue of such a dialectic, as the roots interact with fungi and bacteria, worms and insects in the surrounding soil. This is a dialectic of reaching-out and taking-in.

There is much more we could say about the distinction between the verticality and horizontality of plants, but this initial contrast allows us to see that plants (including trees) present themselves to us as operating according to two fundamental axial principles: verticalizing and horizontalizing. Combinations and compromises between these two principles certainly occur, as when we confront plants whose most conspicuous directionality is neither horizontal nor vertical but diagonal. But we must be cautious here. Any such supposed geometricity overlooks its organic basis, as with the sections of the plant hidden from view in the soil. Such geometricity involves a factor of imposition or projection that is only inconsistently evident in our actual experience of plants. Some plants do seem to stand up high: notably, fully mature palm trees that seem to reach into the heavens. But many plants, including certain species of trees, are much more ambiguous in terms of their primary directionality: they appear to grow in every which way. This feature exhibits some of the same indefiniteness that characterizes the places of plants themselves—places that are only rarely fully flat or circular but are highly variegated in shape and extent.

IV

In the full description of the perceived directionality of plants as of their underlying places, what Peirce called "the logic of the vague" is more apposite than any putative formal axiality. Far from an allusion to such vagueness being a sign of failure to capture the inherent directionality of plants and the character of their emplacements, it is precisely what is most apposite. This is so even if terms like *horizontal* and *vertical* can be useful in a preliminary effort to do descriptive justice to the appearance of plants as we encounter them in daily existence. But these are at most first approximations rather than anything definitive.

To do justice to how plants present themselves in their attachments to earth, we must allow for the way that the firstness of plants and their inherent places enter our lives—*Firstness* being Peirce's term for sheer qualitative presence. Here we must make room for the dense imbroglio that being in the presence of plants can bring with it. We may point to experiences such as being immersed in a field of densely situated plants attached to their places in the earth without any recognizable pattern. This happens whenever one of us (EC) finds himself in the midst of a garden in front of his home in Santa Barbara. This is an informal garden filled with miscellaneous plants of very diverse descriptions, some of which can be seen in this photograph:

Figure 5.1. Home Garden. Photograph by Ali R. Pharaa, October 28, 2021.

There is no obvious ordering principle in this garden, which replaces an earlier lawn that sported grass only. No predesignated pathway leads through it, and the various plants do not follow any plan as to their type: they are a miscellany of quite different kinds. Yet, for those who live in the house to which the garden is attached, it is a coherent and familiar presence. It is referred to merely as "the garden," and the apparent disorder is accepted as integral to its identity.

To be on the porch bordering this informal garden is to be on the edge of a wild scene. The lack of a recognizable order does not mean that the plants are themselves confused; whatever order they may have among themselves, even if not evident to the human eye, is nonetheless *their order*. Such an immanent ordering obtains for even the most seemingly casual commixture of plants. Verticality and horizontality and diagonality are all present, but mainly in recessive ways that are far from conspicuous. In place of a kind of stark presentation, which the perception of a single upstanding plant or tree brings with it, there is something closer to the "blooming, buzzing confusion" of which William James spoke.

The configuration overall is nevertheless not sheerly chaotic. A certain tacit order inheres in the casual conjunction of singular plants. This order underlies the apparent disorder as to kinds of plant, plant sizes, and the placement of individual specimens that make up the garden itself. We are far from the strict regulation that obtains for the king's garden at Versailles and even from the British gardens composed of masses of trees with which Versailles and other formal gardens are often contrasted. Yet there is an emergent order—a unique Firstness at a qualitative level that is not only visual but also experienced by way of scent, the motion of the plants as they sway gently in the breeze, and by the varied ways of being attached to earth through their respective places.

At the edge of this scene, we find ourselves drawn into an enigmatic array that calls for what, as we have already mentioned, Quasha designates as *ecoproprioception*.[3] This is a felt sense of a qualitative wholeness that, no matter how diverse and disordered it may appear to be, nevertheless constitutes something coherent for the person who takes it in. This is not a matter of the subjacent order among the plants but now our own ordering of their order, however implicit this may be as something that does not proceed according to any formal geometric structure. Ecoproprioceptive ordering accounts for the fact that, in the case of the informal home garden in Santa Barbara, we can refer to it as "*the* garden" in a coherent way despite the disarray of its direct presentation. Its Firstness, its sheerly qualitative presence, is rendered as a single spectacle—single enough and coherent enough to serve as exemplary in our brief foregoing discussion of it. Its *it* coheres as one whole despite the initially disarming disarray of its diverse constituents.

The result is a dialectic that operates between the intrinsic ordering of plants among themselves—inapparent as this may be—and our re-ordering of it in ecoproprioception. The latter is not an imposition on the bare presentation of the garden but a gentle shaping of its presence before and around us, helping to make this presentation make sense to us at the level of multisensory perception. As we are unlikely to know the ultimate order of the garden unless we are plant scientists, we must rely on our own ecoproprioceptive powers to experience a single scene that is coherent on our own terms.

This is a scene of attachments—of plants exhibiting various modes of being attached to their places and, through them, to the earth beneath. Without a sure sense of such attachments, we'd be confronted with a shifting and ever-changing scene that would be intrinsically chaotic: not just seemingly so at first glance. Plants would be flying and flowing all over the place—where "place" itself no longer makes sense. In that case, what the Romans called *stabilitas loci* would be lost. Not even the most powerful ecoproprioceptive powers could bring minimal order to such a tumultuous scene: we would be blown away by its blowing itself away.

B. DETACHMENT

I

Plants' rootedness in the earth marks yet another difference between vegetal and animal modes of being. Either at the moment of birth or prior to it (for instance, when eggs are laid), an animal separates from the body of the maternal other. Plants, for their part, maintain the attachment to the earth throughout and beyond their germination, which is an equivalent of birth. But although they are firmly rooted in the earth as the indispensable substratum of their place, plants consist of a relatively loose assemblage of parts, many of which, such as the leaves, the flowers, or the fruit, they let go of in the seasonal cycle and in the cycles of their lives. The regeneration of the earth depends to a great extent on this detachment: rotting into the earth around the trees that shed them, fallen leaves replenish the soil, allowing it to welcome future growth. Entire trunks of dead trees perform the same service for the forest as a whole. What detaches in a step that is neither decisively active nor simply passive (so something that is expressed in the middle voice) is thus taken up again, precisely in the reuptake of nutrients drawn from decomposing vegetal matter.

Likewise, for their reproductive strategies to succeed, plants must vigorously practice the detachment of structures carrying their genetic materials. In his *Philosophy of Nature*, Hegel recognizes that sexual difference emerges in the vegetal kingdom, but he deems it to be "only quite partial" there (*der Unterschied ist so nur ganz partiell*) for two reasons.[4] First, plant sexuality is indeterminate, and "the differences are very often changeable while plants are growing." Second, and more important, this sexuality is concentrated in the flower, a detachable and superfluous part of plant, *ein abgeschiedener Teil*. "The different individuals," Hegel writes on the same page, "cannot therefore be regarded as of different sexes because they have not been completely imbued with the *principle* of their opposition [*sie nicht in daß* Prinzip *ihrer Eingegensetzung ganz eingetaucht find*]—because this does not completely pervade them [*nicht ganz durchbringt*], is not a universal moment of the entire individual." For Hegel, the detachment of plant parts, their nonintegration in an organismic totality is not a sign of freedom, of malleability, playfulness, and plasticity, which we find at the vegetal origins of sexuality, but of evolutionary and, above all, dialectical immaturity.

Whatever one's take on vegetal sexuality, the periodic emergence and detachment of various plant organs counterbalances their rooted attachment to the earth. One feature of what detaches from the "mother plant" is that it moves in a way otherwise foreclosed for the rest of the tree, bush, or flower, which stays rooted, namely by locomotion. To be sure, such movements are not independent, facilitated as they are by flowing water or the wind, by insects or birds. But, intriguingly enough, they also provide a tacit model for conceiving of human populational movements said to be diasporic.

It turns out that the term *diaspora*—one of our main names for the effects of human migration—is a borrowing from botanical discourse, where diaspore refers to seeds or spores, plus the plant's anatomical structures fitted for their dispersal. A fruit with its seeds is a diaspore, as is the white dandelion puff ball and tumbleweed rolling across windswept plains. Diasporic communities form as a consequence of human migratory flows, imagined by analogy to the movement of plants.

What is it that moves and how, when diaspores and diasporas are set loose? At its Greek source, the word indicates the splitting of the scattered. An obvious interpretation of this etymology would be that seed dispersal units, such as ripe fruits ready to fall to the ground, detach from the mother plant, and that human migrants are cut off from their original communities cast in the role of trees that nourished them. There is, however, much more to diaspores and diasporas than initially meets the eye.

II

Detachment is an irrevocable possibility of plants, with many of their parts not only detachable but also "prosthetic," replaceable, ready to be shed without causing harm to those that tentatively stay behind. Further, scatter is not an accident that only belatedly affects the seed; whether we are talking about *spora* or *sperma* (the difference between vegetal, animal, and human reproduction blurred), seed is essentially scatter well before it reaches the ground, is carried by water, or glides on air. Its division into two (*dia-*) seeds (*spora*) and into an infinity that stirs between that which is split into two intensifies the dynamics proper to what is internally, congenitally divided.

The inorganic world gets caught up in the semantics of the diaspore as well, considering that this vegetal invention lends an apt geological designation to a mineral (diasporite, empholite) that, after being heated, breaks up into white pearly scales. But, despite the blurring of boundaries among biological kingdoms and between organic and inorganic realms, vegetal migrations have their distinctive traits. For one, plants use reproductive structures specialized for seed or spore dispersal, whereas animals and humans may journey both in the encrypted form of their DNA, separate from the bodies that have released it, and as "whole" organisms. For another, plants catch a ride on the backs of others: the elements, such as atmospheric movements of air masses; insects wings; the digestive tracts of animals, who will excrete the seeds they have devoured without interfering with their generative, germinal potential.[5] Let us follow each of these two threads and see whither they lead us in their unspooling.

In seeds, spores, and pollen, plants condense themselves, distilling their being into something portable.[6] By and large, they travel light, packing the bare minimum indispensable for future growth elsewhere, the growth that will be shaped by and will eventually shape the seed's landing site. Our migrations are not as flexible. Human migrants stand in need of careful transplanting techniques so as to grow new roots in the soil of another country, culture, place, while abiding between identities, cultures, histories.

Still, the contrast between vegetal parts and human wholes has its limits. If, rather than organs, diaspores are semiautonomous multiplicities, then they are both more and less than an organism. Their simultaneously supra- and infraorganismic makeup allows them to prefigure dispersed communities on the move or, in a word, diasporas. Multiplicity is ingrained in the singularity of a migratory identity, very much in keeping with plants that are one in many and many in one. Migration has to do with population fluxes, and a migrant is a fleeting individuation out of the motile mass, a flickering speck in the scatter of numerous dots. To disregard the primacy of mass movements is to switch attention, surreptitiously, from migrants to itinerant persons and, hence, to depoliticize them.

How plants are dispersed is equally significant, even if instructively different. A diaspore and its contents dropping down to earth or entrusted to the wind, pollen attaching to butterfly wings, or seeds wending their way to another place in the stomachs of birds—all these acts are awash with the contingencies of carrying and of landing. In throwing themselves, in opening themselves up to dis- or relocation, plants throw their fates to the winds and to chance. As a compensation for the uncertainty of the outcome, they increase the number of throws, following a near infinity of possible trajectories, some of them bound to succeed where a vast majority fail. This is luxury not available to a human migrant.

In truth, the categories of success and failure only make sense upon arrival at a destination, however unexpected that terminal point may be. The logic of arrival is foreign to diaspora and migration. Neither an emigrant nor an immigrant, a migrant, like a mobile diaspore, is suspended in the in-between after departure and before arrival. For many, most recently in the Mediterranean basin or in the desert between Mexico and the U.S., the suspension has proven deadly. It put them in limbo, in a broken transit line with no end in sight, both finite and infinite, the "Middle Passage," as Édouard Glissant christened it with regard to forced migrations in the transatlantic slave trade. (It bears mentioning here that okra seeds migrated to the New World across the Middle Passage, concealed in the hair of African slaves.) But even those who safely reach the desired shores are not free from the uncanny interval containing in itself the entire phenomenon of migration in miniature. Awaiting their transplantation, human migrants, again like seeds and pollen, migrate in their afterlife, which is also their before-life: a stretch, a span as temporal as it is spatial.

Their scattering at the beginning and in the end notwithstanding, human migratory flows display determinate patterns and follow clearly identifiable vectors. People flee from extreme danger and scarcity to perceived safety, plentiful resources, and the promise of well-being, if not of happiness. Plants, too, can respond to perilous situations (of being under attack by herbivories) by initiating physiological, morphological, or other changes in themselves, and they can grow deliberately toward the resources that are vital for them, including sunlight, moisture, and minerals. But when they release their genetic material, to be carried by the wind or by bees, they do not calculate the trajectory of the throw and refrain from choosing an optimal vector for the realization of their procreative goals. Unless they do so at a transgenerational, evolutionary level, for instance, by optimizing the timing and the efficiency of the release of pollen or spurs or by increasing the attractiveness of flowers to pollinators.[7]

IV

German and French philosophical traditions, including among others Kant, Friedrich Schiller, and Hegel, as well as Georges Bataille and Jacques Derrida, to whose *dissemination* we feel incredibly close (what is *dissemination*, if not the Latinized rendering of the Greek *diaspora*?), have framed the vegetal wager as excessive and immoderate, a surfeit over and above the economic logic of investment-and-return, as though the throw were "for nothing." This eccentric behavior is strange only in the eyes of an ideally autonomous, self-sufficient human subject. Vegetal heteronomy means that, having been thrown and in all probability thrown *away*, the seed retraces, outside the usual pitting of activity against passivity, in a sort of lived middle voice, the pathways of others, from the elements to the swarms of insects and flocks of birds. Plants are collaborative, synergetic beings, which is why their migratory itineraries rehearse and reaffirm the large-scale movements of air masses, of the retreating ice sheets, or of animal and human populations.

An additional complication in the story of migration surfaces, as if exposed by the melting Arctic ice or floating on the waves of the rising seas in the age of climate change. Membership in the category *environmental refugees*, encompassing not only humans but also plants, animals, fungi, and myriads of other forms of life, is increasing as global temperatures rise. Displaced populations of all kinds are on the move. Climate change is one of the elemental forces, akin to wind, driving human migrations, in contravention to the belief that humanity has finally managed to dominate and subdue the capricious and destructive powers of nature.

The unfolding global environmental catastrophe, spawning masses of refugees, cannot be reduced to the displacement of vegetal, human, animal populations from their native habitats. It affects the very notion of place and its relation to placelessness. It turns out that the livable character of the world—whoever it is a world *for*—has been ensured by the largely unlivable, iced over swathes of the earth and the ocean that have globally kept climates and ocean levels relatively stable. On a planetary scale, circumscribed placelessness has guaranteed the relative stability of places. The climate emergency means that *stabilitas loci* is severely undermined today, so much so that places themselves are, also and in the first instance, on the move. Moreover, the migration of places is toward the condition of placelessness, which, no longer circumscribed, is unchained and generalized, thwarting the conditions of habitability that make a place the attractive and viable place it is.

Given the fitful history of life on the planet, we find some hope in our dire predicament: our consolation is that, though no longer suitable for us, a place may still be propitious to the lives of others, notably of other-than-human forms of life. Under the banner of ecological resilience, helping to make an unmitigated disaster palatable, plants are the main protagonists. Their plasticity is remarkable at the physiological and epigenetic levels, enabling vegetation to adapt to ionizing radiation and to resist environmental mutagens better, more efficiently than we humans do. Plants survived Chernobyl; fresh, brilliantly green shoots are not long in sprouting after devastating and ever more frequent forest fires; and grasses and weeds make their comeback to the postindustrial wastelands. They come to embody in this manner the miraculous, phoenix-like attributes humans have been imputing to the natural environment since times immemorial, the attributes according to which no matter the severity of the violence our species unleashes onto the planet, ecosystems will regenerate and the "circle of life" will begin gyrating once again.

The projection of a world without human beings where quasi-paradisiac nature will be recovered thanks to vegetal diasporas is a hard-to-resist temptation. Migrating seeds will accidentally fall on polluted or burnt soil, near contaminated rivers and lakes, and redeem the ravished earth, cutting short the increasing placelessness of humans and other animals. And yet, ongoing regeneration occurs within fragile and relatively narrow limits that are currently under severe threat. Seeds that have just fallen in the cracks of concrete have a chance to germinate at this moment in time. But will the odds be the same by the end of the century when droughts, excessively high temperatures, and depleted soils will be the global rule rather than an exception? In a 2014 report, the UN warned that, assuming current rates of degradation, most of the planet's topsoil could be gone by 2075.[8] The alarming prospect is that the earth has just over fifty years of crops to give before becoming infertile. In other words, vegetal detachment may not be an infinitely renewable, replenishable gift, its contents to be taken up again in the process of plant nourishment and growth.

In truth, the entire earth is caught up in a cycle of generation and degeneration that, at the level of plants, can be regarded as an ecodrama of attachment and detachment. Plants are attached in a myriad labyrinthine ways to the earth through their root systems, which are the basis of their emplacement. But they are also detached from the earth through the diaspora of their seeds, realizing highly adaptable and ingenious ways of continuing to exist even in the face of the planet's increasing environmental havoc.

On the one hand, attachment to the earth generates a sure sense of concrete place, even if this place eludes precise measurement. On the other hand, detachment as we have discussed it, entails a certain placelessness in the period of the sheer dispersion of seeds. Yet significant numbers of these seeds settle somewhere in particular, and, fragile as it may be, a new place emerges. This new home can be very diversely situated, but it counts as a place of residence, much as it may be short-lived. Even in the extremities of detachment, place arises from what is temporarily placeless, however tenuous its generation and eventual survival. Every form of life on earth is transitional from one mode of being emplaced to another: place is always at stake, despite the diversity of the ways in which it can emerge and despite the fact that it can come to exist from placelessness itself.

CONCLUSION
The Fate of Places, the Fate of Plants

I

In the course of this brief book, we have encountered the issue of the place of plants many times. We have seen that such a place brings with it a paradoxical dimension whereby it is requisite on the one hand and yet quite indeterminate on the other. Every plant is emplaced and has its own location on earth or in the sea (and sometimes even in the air): it is found *somewhere*—a very particular somewhere that is the very place of a particular plant, *its* place: *where it is*. This place can be shared to some extent, as when we notice two bushes growing out of the same small piece of ground. Their branches commingle, and so do their roots. In this case, the place is bivalent, serving two plants at once (or the same plant that appears before our visual first impression as being two). Still, it presents itself as *one place*, a single and singular patch whose topmost layer is manifest in the soil that lies just under the double plant and whose lower layers are continuous with this visible part even if they are not accessible to sight, often complicated by the presence of the root systems of still other plants or by rocks buried in the soil, streamlets of water, etc. Despite the complexity of its material composition, it remains one place, *this place,* the place for the two interbraided plants. It is at once *unique*—this place and no other—and *necessary*: a placeless plant cannot last for long. If we tear a plant out of its place in the ground, we need to replant it in soil somewhere else for it to survive.

In these diverse ways and still others, places prove essential to the life of plants, however variable their emplacement may be in given instances. Yet the same places resist being determined by standard measurements. Is the place of the rose bush in front of me 2.5 feet by 3 feet? So I might estimate casually and at first glance. But I know this is a merely approximate guess. If I get out a measuring stick and apply it to the ground at the base of the rose bush, I soon realize the absurdity of any such effort: putting a ruler on the ground will not tell me what the true dimensions of the place of the bush are. Soon I realize that a plant's place as it presents itself to me will not submit to such numerical determination. Although I can refer to it as "this place" or "the place of the rose bush" in a quite intelligible way—if I utter these words, my friend who stands next to me will well understand what I mean—I cannot intelligibly say: it is 2 feet and 3 inches wide and 1 foot and 7.5 inches long (measurements that are applicable to a niche for a desk in my office or for a bed in the bedroom): or if I do, my friend will look at me incredulously as if I were speaking perfect nonsense. Which indeed I would be. The language of inches and feet is not only inappropriate, it is deeply misguided. It shows me looking for what is not there.

In short, about a rose bush in whose company I find myself, I can say unequivocally: *There it is*; or, if I draw close to it, *Here it is.* But I cannot say *just where it is.* The *here* and the *there* are determined by my felt proximity to the plant; but the just-where is a matter of belonging to world space—the space of a world that is known and measured in determinate units. This is a world that is indifferent to what occupies it: whether it be humans or plants or animals—in such a world, everything is subject to exact measurement in such units. This is part of a modernist mania for what Whitehead calls "simple location." But the locations, the places, of organic beings such as plants are not simple; even for a single plant they are densely complex, their indeterminacy symptomatic of the indeterminacy of life—not (only) of life in general but of the vitality uniquely singularized in this rose bush. We do not even know just where they begin or end in terms of the space they occupy on and in the ground: they are in effect *lost in space*. Not knowing just where they are positioned in space, how can we ascribe numbers to them? Places are not parts of spaces, and they do not possess attributes that, in the manner of simple location, are characterizable in numerical terms.

The paradox deepens: we can intelligibly say a plant is here or there—and even point to the place it is in—yet we cannot say just where it stops or starts, much less what the exact dimensions of its being here or there are, nor, due to the sessility of vegetal organisms, where the plant itself ends and its place begins. "There the rose bush is," we say gesturing to it from where we stand; and when we draw close enough to it, we can intelligibly say, "here it is." But this interchangeability of the locatory adverbs *here* and *there* is largely a function of where our bodies are in relation to the plant in question, although there is a partial overlap of the *here* of my body now seated under an old olive tree and the *there* of the tree itself. They have no exact dimensions of their own, nor do they designate anything stably measured. I can say "here" when standing over the plant and hovering just above it or when suspended further and further above this plant: on and on without definite limit. So too I can intelligibly say "there" from an indefinite multiplicity of locations, no one of which is privileged. In all such locations, I speak intelligibly for those who can hear me and do not need to offer them any more precise designations: "it is over there," I say, pointing to the plant, and few will ever ask me to say just how far away I am. And if I say, "it is about three feet from here," it is evident that I am not alluding to any discrete distance but to a sense that the plant in question is relatively close to where I stand: where the use of "relatively" signifies that I am not pretending to make any definite measurement but using "three feet" as a signifier for something that is not exactly three feet away—which is to say, not just that far away.

II

We can designate this paradox as that of the definite and the indefinite. A plant is definitely here or there, yet we cannot say just where its place is with any recognizable numerical exactitude (also due to the ongoing movements of growth, decay, and metamorphosis whereby the plant changes continually along with its very place). Determining its exact extent is not only elusive; it is unspecifiable—at least not in the exact measuring units that have become pervasive in modernity. These units proved useful in the determination of plots of land—increasingly designated as "real estate" with the rise of capitalism and the associated disappearance of the commons, a place meant to be shared among people and animals and plants. The ever-increasing quantification of land also came paired with the disappearance of open land. At stake here was the triumph of the assumption that to be located is to be situated somewhere that is of measurable extent. In this way, *place became site*. Not that place itself vanished. Far from it: it remained indispensably present for all sentient beings, whose experience on earth is irrevocably placial.

For place is an indispensable dimension of all ecoproprioceptive experience; but the recognition of its role in the machinations of the modern world became increasingly diminished by a focus on site-specific concerns: the clocking of exact working hours arose alongside a precise determination of the spatial extent of the factories in which human labor was quantified in temporal terms. And, as hi-tech and concomitant digitalization have increasingly come to invade so many dimensions of everyday life, the triumph of the measurable has been ever more ascendant.

All this was nowhere more evident than in the gradual but concerted effort to convert place into site—where "site" signifies location that is intrinsically measurable. By now it should be evident that it is sitification that underlies the paradox just discussed. Without the valorization of measurement, the resistance of place to its numerical determination would not appear significant. But now we realize that this resistance was to be expected. Taking account of early modernity's obsession with measurability, we can see how the effort to measure place was foredoomed. Indeed, we realize that the effort was misguided from the start, though it left long shadows that still haunt anyone wishing to take place seriously and to understand it on its own terms.

III

It is time to recognize that plants are game changers when it comes to matters of place. The fate of plants themselves may well include their commodification, as when they are put up for sale in plant markets. But this appropriation for commercial purposes does not undermine the basic belonging of plants to earth, thanks to their unique emplacements on the planet and of the many ways they both rely on and gradually refashion their places both beneath and above ground level. It cannot be denied that the long arm of capitalism reaches into the midst of the plant world, as when crop monocultures are cultivated at the expense of vegetal diversity, trees are cut down to supply lumber, or plants are arranged in floral shops for weddings and other occasions. But the places of plants themselves retain an integrity that is much less often the case with places as inhabited and experienced by humans. Where the latter places are all too often subject to efforts to quantify and measure them—and to "improve" them—the places of plants remain remarkably impervious to sitification, affirming themselves as *placial on their own multivalent terms*. Getting clear on what such placiality means has been a major objective of this book. The aim is to understand what it is about the place of plants that is unique and specific to them, however vulnerable such places may be not only due to the challenges of catastrophic climate change and to the depletion of topsoils and of carbon-absorbing forests around the world but also to those of existence in an intensely quantifying civilization, such as our own, in which there is a pervasive mania of measurement.[1]

Our strategy in this book has been to *let plants take the lead* in matters of place. Indeed, they are already in the lead if we can bring ourselves to acknowledge their priority in such matters, counterintuitive as it may seem to be. After at least a billion years of evolution (when the first eukaryotes, or green plants, emerged), the plants' thriving in the places of their growth has rendered the world ever more inhabitable for vegetal and nonvegetal species alike; after only two or three hundred thousand years of the evolution of *Homo sapiens*, the planet's livability is under a severe threat because of the effects of anthropogenic climate change. And yet, all too often we assume that plants are somehow more primitive than animals, especially human animals:

a claim of Aristotle's that still resonates today. But we now know this is far from being the case. If anything, plants surpass humans in their intricately interlocked intelligence; at the very least, we should "admit that intelligence is something we have in common with all other species of animals and plants."[2] The fact that this intelligence takes different forms in plants and humans in no way lessens its significance. If we are ready to recognize intelligence among other primates, why should we not extend the same recognition to plants?[3]

IV

Our contentions in this book point to two major conclusions:

> The fate of plants is tied to the places they occupy.
> The fate of the place of human beings and of other animal species is intrinsically and intimately linked to plants' emplacement.

Let us say something about each of these fateful circumstances. Both concern the fate of place: what it means, its significance for plants, humans, and other animals. Until very recently, and then only in passing, little has been said about place in the context of plant life. For the most part—with rare exceptions—it has been overlooked or, more likely, taken for granted. This oversight is due in considerable measure to the immeasurability of place, as just discussed. The modernist assumption is that if something is not measurable, either it does not exist or it can be safely overlooked. As immeasurable, place is just such a thing; as an all too predictable consequence, it has become neglected in the modern era: either ignored or assumed to be of minor consequence. No wonder we read so little about the place of plants, themselves neglected until recently by philosophers, especially since early modernity. That said, place is essential to the life and well-being of plants. Elusive as it may seem to be, plants could not exist without it, nor could most places be inhabitable without plants.

In other words, *there is no placeless plant.* Plants' places come in many guises, but they are always present in one form or another, ranging from a steady location in a patch of soil right underfoot to a shifting pocket of water in the depths of a sea. The very fact of placial variety matches the diversity of plant species and their very particular needs. Thus, we should not let the apparent straightforwardness of places situated in the familiar soil of our home garden blind us to the proliferation of places occupied by plants far outside this local space. Were there only one viable kind of place, the sheer variety of plants would itself be radically limited. Yet we know that this variety is vast—estimated at nearly four hundred and fifty thousand species just in the case of land plants—and it follows that their characteristic places are comparably numerous. Linking them is a shared resistance to any standard determination in terms of size or shape.

In other words, *there is no Platonic place for plants*: no ideal mode of emplacement, a uniform paradigm, a vegetal *topos ouranios* that is then variously applied here-below. But in keeping with what we can call *the imperative of place* we can say that each living plant calls for a place of its own in which to germinate, grow, and flourish—and eventually to die, to decompose into, and enrich the soil of that place. Indeed, there would be no plants at all without their own attendant places: places in which to become the plants they are meant to be according to their DNA in interaction with the local environments in which they are situated. These are places sufficiently capacious in which to take root and grow: minimally but essentially this much of a place, not more and not less. (Sometimes the placial minimalism of plants is quite astonishing: for instance, when seeds germinate in the lower portion of a wooden window frame, grow between cracks of concrete, or flourish between the slabs of an ancient wall.) But the "much" here is not specifiable in centimeters. All we can say is that it should be adequate and sufficient, without needing to quantify it further. A plant's own place is *there* as its essential locatory base; despite its indeterminacy of exact extent, we can point to it and discuss it intelligibly as "*the* place of *this* plant."

All of this indicates that plants require emplacement and that the fate of plants depends on it. Their specificity as to type of plant, including the form of its branches and the type of its leaves, require such emplacement as sine qua non. The emplacement itself will vary in keeping with several parameters: the character of the plant's material base (soil, water, etc.), the local ecoclimate, interactions with the surrounding species of plants, insects, microorganisms, and the idiosyncrasies of a given plant. These various parameters and still others indicate that the determination of the place of a plant is complex, even if not quantitatively determinable with metric precision. This place is overdetermined: specifiable in the ways we have mentioned and doubtless in still others, such as "secondary qualities" like configuration and texture, all these having to do with the exposed surface of the place. This is not to mention the materiality, indeed the basic elementality of the place itself as earthly, aqueous, aerial, or, in many instances, a mix of the three.

V

If the fate of plants depends on the places they occupy so diversely and indispensably, the fate of place itself—in all its many avatars—depends on plants. Plants not only rely upon the places they occupy so fittingly; these places themselves are animated by the plants that take root in them. At first blush, this seems to be an unlikely claim. How can something so seemingly lifeless as a place—a sheer *there*—call for plants in all their diversity and complexity in order to thrive? Yet places are rendered vital by the plants that inhabit them. For one thing, plants bring with them an entire underworld of fungi and bacteria—a mass of "entangled life" in Sheldrake's phrase—that animate this underworld. This means that such subterranean places are enlivened by what plants bring with them—a congeries of diverse forms of life and nutrient-rich soil into which previous generations of plants or even parts of living plants, such as their fallen leaves, have decomposed. Thanks to this bequest, the places in which plants are situated are lively scenes of activities that are both intensive and extensive: intensive in terms of the intimate interaction thereby generated in the place itself and extensive in terms of the ongoing and outgoing interaction of its often-concealed inhabitants.

So, too, the kind of places that emerge conspicuously aboveground—such as clusters of bushes, groves of trees—depend on a special kind of "sociality," which we have examined earlier in chapter 4. They draw to and around themselves particular species of animals, birds, and insects that find shelter in them, feed on them, and spread their seeds or pollen around them. In such expansive sociality, the formation and shape of places—on-the-ground places we can observe at a distance or explore up close—are a function of the ways that plants communicate among themselves and with members of other biological kingdoms. In the case of trees, aboveground interactive placiality, different as it is from what goes on in underground places, depends on how such trees seek out as well as create a particular interemplacement that constitutes what we call a copse or woods. Similarly aboveground, trees shape the atmosphere, releasing large amounts of humidity into it through their transpiration and oxygen that is the by-product of photosynthesis. It is at their initiative and in their interest that they give rise to their own unique way of being emplaced together and to the microclimates surrounding them. For not just any place will do: rose bushes will not flourish in the desert. Such bushes will flourish best when they are situated securely in soil and configure and energize that soil in very particular ways. Similarly for countless other cases: the places of many plants depend not just on their own nutritional and otherwise supportive character, but they themselves as characteristic and propitious places reflect the kinds of plants that emerge from them. We witness here not only how plants thrive in suitable places and climates but how certain places themselves gain life and character from the plants that have come to be located in them.

This is not to deny that the same soil, or stretch of water, may suit various kinds of plants that together share a place—as in forests or in many informal gardens that feature the close coadunation of plants of very different types, all in one composite place. The same is true for a single bank of soil at a public garden that features diverse species of cacti coexisting with jonquils and a date palm. In such a case, the complex coemplacement reflects the multiplicity of plant life located on it: its placial diversity echoes that of the diversity of plants burrowing into this same soil. The composite character of these plants serves to modulate and shape the place they coinhabit while materially mediating between the earth and the sky without compartmentalizing them into separate regions.

In this concluding set of remarks, we are making a case for the *covalence* of places and plants. One entails the other, and the other entails the one. Between places and plants there is coentailment, which is not a secondary, dispensable feature but the very *fate* of both. Each calls for the other—not merely contingently but coinherently. There are no placeless plants—even if the exact modality of viable places for a given plant may be quite various. And there are few plantless places on the earth as a whole. In situations where there are no plants, there is open space, but nothing that can be seriously considered as *place*. A single juniper cactus in a vast desert not only calls for place, it *is* a place—the very place of the cactus that gives it life and identity. More generally, just as a plant calls for a place in which it can take root, place calls for inhabitation in it by something living—some actual living being. In particular, the rooted character of plants calls for a place in which to be located, a place to be populated on a more or less steady, ongoing basis. Nomads move from place to place; they live in their very circulation between places regarded as temporary residences in a larger cycle of multiple emplacement. But plants are something else: they do not move between places; as individual specimens they stay in one place, even though as a species they can spread their genetic materials far and wide. They are active in that place, bringing it to a level of generativity and vitality not otherwise possible on earth: they endow it with what Bergson called *élan vital*. Just as places give to plants somewhere to be—to subsist in iterative and reliable ways—so plants are *dynamic and enlivening presences in those same places.*

We are not claiming that plants are the sole basis for activating places. Bacteria and other microorganisms as well as humans and other animals do so in their own characteristic ways: for instance, humans by building on them or pursuing agriculture with them or walking through them; animals by seeking refuge in them. Birds certainly activate the places they inhabit—building nests there, returning there to rest, spreading seeds, and hunting for worms and insects on their surfaces, thereby activating them in distinctive ways. But we *are* claiming that plants offer paradigm cases for the activation of places. This is largely due to their settling into places so insistently and for such considerable lengths of time; they quite literally *dig into* them and *take root* there while also renewing the elemental aspects of the places where they are: the soil and the atmosphere. There is a manifest coordination happening here, plants and their places being closely and literally cooperative throughout their coexistence—even in the vegetal afterlife of decay. Together, they realize a unique kind of symbiosis that works to the benefit of each.

Given that place itself is dynamic and not merely inert, we have here an intense dialectical situation in which plants and places not only call for each other, they *require one another*. Neither would be fully what it is—including what it can be—without the other. We are speaking of a situation of interanimation between the place-world and the plant-world. The two worlds not only complement each other; they coalesce in merging to form a deeply covalent ongoing circumstance: that of *plants in place*.

VI

The history of the intellectual and practical depreciation of plants in Western metaphysics (long since incorporated into the opinions of "common sense") consistently spotlighted vegetal immobility. While dismissing out of hand the subtler and slower movements of growth, decay, and metamorphosis, the attribution of immobility to plants focused on their sessility, their rootedness in a place and the impossibility to leave it without dying.

The absence of locomotion in the repertoire of plant behaviors (and so their unconditional attachment to their places of growth) was then taken to be one of the signs of their ontological deficiency, including the absence of reason, voice, sensation, and concern as well as many other supposedly privative attributes of vegetal existence.

For our purposes, it is quite telling that the negative evaluation of plant sessility was understood as being tethered to the place of growth—as if that place were some kind of prison, internally unchangeable, ever the same. A more basic assumption, uniting plants with places and refusing to recognize the dynamism of both, is that places, too, are immobile: a plant is always in its place, and a place is always in place! (In this book, we have alluded to how this assumption trembles not only when the shifting intensities and inner movements of a place become apparent but also, more troublingly, when global climate change displaces the places that it affects on a par with their human and other-than-human populations.) With the rise of modernity, and particularly with the transition from feudalism to capitalism—which unsettled large human groups and opposed itself to the agrarian mode of production—sessility, sedentariness, and attachment to the land (of plants and people associated with them in the places of their growth) were colored with negative hues. That is to say: by virtue of historical vicissitudes as much as by biological necessity, the fate of plants has been inextricably bound to the fate of the places they inhabit.

In light of the current re- or transvaluation of values occasioned, on the one hand, by the collapse of Western metaphysics—already foreseen by Nietzsche in the nineteenth century—and, on the other, by the global environmental crisis, the change of fortunes as far as plants and places are concerned must happen in tandem. The paradox is that, having been taken for granted, depreciated, rendered uniform (within limits), and submitted to the exigencies of an unrestrained instrumental rationality, places and the plants inhabiting them can now be rediscovered in all their richness and cruciality for existence on this planet when they are both endangered, driven to the verge of extinction.

VII

The shared fate of plants and places is also apparent in the linguistic roots that give rise to these English words via Greek and Latin. It is important to mention that the words we use are not *just* words; they are the monuments of bygone thought, and monuments of a special kind, too—living and continually changing, even as, like the growth rings of a tree trunk, they preserve the memories of past traumas and promises. Thus, treating etymology as a symptom—however speculative its interpretation—a brief reflection attuned to the common Greco-Roman origination of *plants* and *places* is in order.

As we have already mentioned, both words derive from the Greek *platus* ("spreading," "broad"), which was converted later into the Latin *planta*, the word for plant and for the sole of a foot. The same etymology is discernable in *place*, as well as in the derivative *plaza* (*piazza, praça* . . .), a public square. In Greek, another linguistic shape of *platus* is *plateia*—"a broad way." (The nickname "Plato" and the inclusion of plane trees in the genus *Platanus* ascend to the same root.)[4]

Why this very brief etymological excursus?

First, it demonstrates the partial, if not biased, understanding of plants and places ingrained in the very linguistic texture of these terms. Indeed, broadness is a necessary feature of both plants and places; it bespeaks the spreading out of a place that supports, as on a stage, everyone and everything taking place there and of the extension of plant parts in their growth. A place must be minimally broad or expansive to accommodate whomever it is a place for. (And it bears reiterating that this accommodating broadness is not objectively measurable; were it to be measurable, it would have turned the place into a container for the dead, a casket. Rather, the expansiveness of a place is broad enough to receive and potentiate a vibrant relational ensemble of life in that place.) Be it as slim as a blade of grass, a plant in turn must be broad enough—and periodically broadening by way of vegetative growth—to receive, among other things, solar energy on the surface of its leaves. But while broadness is a necessary feature of places and plants alike, it is insufficient. Both are inconceivable without depth and heterogeneity, a rooting in the soil, which does not fit the quality of flatness in the case of plants and the infinitely adumbrated unevenness in the case of places. If plants and places are akin to a theatrical stage for the appearing—of events, of beings, of life itself—then they are stages replete with a backstage and wings, with parts that *do not* appear in the open and, in their not-appearing, make that which does appear possible.

Second, the flatness that the words for plants and places hint at is not only ontic—a quality of a surface without notable protrusions or differences in height—but also ontological: a flattening of the very *being* of places and plants. Nothing mysterious or numinous, such a flattening is also a leveling (down). It is the outcome of an activity—that of preparing a plot of land for cultivation by making it arable, of creating a city square or a broad thoroughfare, of felling trees, of making sure that the terrain roughly corresponds to and offers support to the flat sole of the human foot, the sole that is also, as noted, called *planta* in Latin. Flattened plants, well before the advent of contemporary monocultures, are those that have been homogenized, "domesticated," and are thereby primed for growing as crops. And, assuming that the first human communities in history settled around the fields of cereals they cultivated, anthropogenic plant and place flatness have been mutually reinforced for millennia. Although the categories plants and places need to be as general as possible (that is to say, not pre-specified as to the kinds of places or plants that are included in them), they unwittingly betray the prior work of determination and delimitation—the work we have called *flattening*, with which the words designating them are stamped.

Since plants and places have been flattened down, surreptitiously determined as to the kinds of plants and places they are within purportedly nondetermined (indeed "broad") categories, and homogenized in advance both linguistically and conceptually, the task of philosophies and practices concerned with their fate—and thus with the fate of a livable planet—is to recover their heterogeneity, their diversity irreducible even to the many vegetal species or to the multiple types of places that, at the very least, as we have argued, matches the diversity of species. Spatially speaking—though, without a doubt, these terms overflow their spatial sense into experiential and axiological domains—the challenge is to reintegrate the horizontality, verticality, and laterality of plants and places (and of plants in their places) into that endlessly heterogeneous commixture we call nature.

VIII

The tasks and challenges just mentioned sound quite heady and daunting; yet they do not—not actively at any rate—seek out either "special places" invested with larger-than-life significance in cultural imagination or rare species of plants. At a practical level, we can take up these challenges by returning to the places we already know and reengaging with the common plants that surround us. We may do so by paying renewed attention to the experience of being in place and to the plants that share and, indeed, invest placiality with meaning through their particular mode of fidelity to a place, namely sessility. To return—mindfully, attentively, caringly—to the places where we already are is also, and by the same token, to return 1. to the plants, whose places they are in a different way, partially overlapping with ours; and 2. to ourselves as emplaced beings. That this overlap is partial implies that, appealing as it may seem, the plants' being-in-place cannot serve as a model for human placial experience, although the differently emplaced character of both may chart the way to an auspicious meeting of vegetal and human existences.

The manifold ramifications of returning to the places where we are—which are also, if differently and in the first instance, the places of plants—indicate a positive (and inexhaustible, despite its finitude) overflow of meaning that bubbles up from that meeting. Plants and places excel in semiotic or biosemiotic excess: in their mutual immanence, they point to a welter of beings they gather in or around them—including their proximity to each other. Quite literally, *plants in place* are uncontainable, ontically and ontologically untamable. And the immanence of places—of being in place—is similarly distinct from the notion of containment that is for Aristotle the primary characteristic of a place. It is a matter of recognizing the elastic and indeterminate boundaries of places such as we have discussed throughout this book.

The relation between plants and places is a two-way street: in addition to growing in the places in which they are rooted, plants can themselves *be* places, that is to say, habitats for other plants, insects, birds, squirrels and other small arboreal-dwelling mammals. The unavoidable ambiguity of a term such as *plant habitats* reflects a fold in habitation, around which activity and passivity converge. Plants are, simultaneously, the inhabiting and the inhabited, grounds and figures, the *wherein* of habitation and its tenants, beings in place and places. As a result, life no longer appears as an undifferentiated ground in contrast to the living figures who stand out from it. In plant habitats, the dance of figure and ground continues indefinitely, with plants occupying both positions interchangeably or all at once: as plants *and* places, or plants *with* places, the two indissolubly intermixed.

We have thus reached a point at which plants may be envisioned as places while themselves remaining in place, but can we imagine places as kinds of plants? Such a line of thinking is plausible, since the internal dynamism of places is of a piece with the movement of plants: places, too, can grow extensively or intensively, decay, and metamorphose. Should we follow such an argument, we would be recollecting an ancient insight on the *functional analogism* of beings rather than their morphological similarities: for instance, the consideration of fire as a sublime animal or a plant, born of a spark, capable of reproducing itself, moving across the terrain and, finally, dying out.[5] The planthood of places and the placeness of plants are the two exceptional instances of a convergence that are worth exploring further.

Nevertheless, our goal in this book has not been to equate plants with places and places with plants, even if, in some cases, such an equation is possible. *Plants in Place* has been an attempt to tease out the *relation* between these two vital but, until recently, philosophically neglected notions or figures while also juxtaposing this relation to that of humans to our places and to plants. Now, a relation, however coinherent its terms, is an affinity where the limits of the *relata* do not disappear, fused into a greater whole, but come into view with greater vividness. Just as vegetal life exhibits the cobelonging of attachment and detachment, so relations of all kinds are made of unity and separation, of bonds and their unbinding, necessitating the ongoing work of tying and retying them over and over again. The invitation we have extended to each other as authors and to the readers of our book to think through and reexperience the relation between plants and places has focused on close affinities between these two relata: within the field of possibilities or possibilitization; with respect to intensive movement and other such dynamisms; concerning the sense of the stability of what is *here* and the prospects of displacement or dislocation over *there*; as well as affinities, as we have just seen, at the level of language.

Throughout these reflections, we have not *reduced* plants to places, or vice versa, but endeavored to tie, untie, and retie the vibrant relations between them. In doing this, we have in effect returned to our guiding questions: How can the thinking and experience of place be enriched starting from the places of plants? How can a vegetal mode of being be better appreciated starting from the emplacement of plants as sessile, yet growing, decaying, metamorphosing beings? The more we contemplate them, the clearer the realization that these two questions are inexhaustible—that the relations of plants and places demand not a further conceptual tightening but an unfaltering untying and retying.

NOTES

PREFACE

1. Rousseau, of course, was known for collecting herbaria, but, in his epistolary confession to Margaret Cavendish, the Duchess of Portland, he states his preference for moving as freely as an insect or to herborize as well as a sheep in an attempt to free himself from the constraints of his human identity in the company of plants. Refer to Jean-Jacques Rousseau, *Collected Writings*, vol. 8: *The Reveries of the Solitary Walker, Botanical Writings, and Letter to Franquières*, ed. C. Kelly (Hanover, N.H.: University Press of New England, 2000), p. 174.
2. On the dynamics of root life, see Stefano Mancuso and Alessandra Viola, *Bright Green: The Surprising History and Science of Plant Intelligence* (Washington, D.C.: Island, 2015), pp. 140 ff., esp. p. 145: "lacking a specific organ to supervise cognitive functions, plants developed a form of distributed intelligence [in their root system], typical of swarms."
3. There are, as always, a few exceptions to this rule. The most notable is the stilt palm, which we will revisit further down the line.
4. See Seong-Yun Park and Richard Mattson, "Ornamental Indoor Plants in Hospital Rooms Enhanced Health Outcomes of Patients Recovering from Surgery," *National Library of Medicine*, https://pubmed.ncbi.nlm.nih.gov/19715461/.
5. For a detailed discussion on Rousseau and botany, consult Alexandra Cook, *Jean-Jacques Rousseau and Botany: The Salutary Science* (Oxford: Voltaire Foundation—University of Oxford, 2012).

6. Gary Snyder, "The Etiquette of Freedom" in *The Practice of the Wild* (Washington, D.C.: Shoemaker and Hoard, 1990), p. 19.
7. Snyder.
8. See Mary Watkins, *Mutual Accompaniment and the Creation of the Commons* (New Haven: Yale University Press, 2019).
9. This is the subtitle of chapter 2 of Snyder, *The Practice of the Wild*, as cited in the book's index.
10. Snyder, p. 29.
11. Tellingly, the inattentive and a priori dismissive attitudes to plants also relate to them as to green blur, rendering those who harbor such attitudes passenger-like, even when they (or we) are not on public or semi-public means of transport.
12. Michael Marder, *Philosophy for Passengers* (Cambridge, Mass. MIT Press, 2022), p. 97.
13. See the essay by this title by Megan Craig and Edward Casey in Ron Scapp and Brian Seitz, eds., *Philosophy, Travel, and Place: Being in Transit* (New York: Palgrave and Macmillan, 2018).

1. THE PLACIAL BASIS OF PLANT SESSILITY AND MOBILITY

1. For an account of the suffering of solitary confinement, see Lisa Guenther, *Solitary Confinement: Social Death and Its Afterlives* (Minneapolis: University of Minnesota Press, 2013). Guenther describes the penury of what she labels as "social death" and "civil death" that accompanies such confinement.
2. There are other sessile beings such as mollusks, but for plants immobility is the rule. For economy's sake, we shall refer mainly to *plants* as a generic term that includes trees as well as other living beings hard to classify by the usual categories of recognized life on earth. Certain parts of our work will attend to trees as such.
3. Richard Karban, "Plant Behavior and Communication," *Ecology Letters 11* (2008), p. 728, pp. 728–39, doi: 10.1111/j.1461-0248.2008.01183.x.
4. Michael Marder, *Plant-Thinking: A Philosophy of Vegetal Life* (New York: Columbia University Press, 2013), introduction.
5. Human mobility, on which we concentrate here, is of course only an instance of a far more widespread *animal* mobility. This is not to

overlook that there are inherent mobilities of other living things—-
e.g., fungi and bacteria and insects, which move at their own velocities.
6. "Plant," in *An Etymological Dictionary of the English Language*, ed. Walter W. Skeat (Oxford: Clarendon, 1888), p. 448.
7. See Erik Bormanis and Edward S. Casey, "Places of Belonging—and Not Belonging," forthcoming in Danielle Petherbridge, ed., *The Phenomenology of Belonging* (New York: State University of New York Press, 2023).
8. G. W. F. Hegel, *Phenomenology of Spirit*, translated by A. V. Miller (Oxford: Oxford University Press, 1977), pp. 60–61.
9. MM discusses this feature in his book on "passengerhood," titled *Philosophy for Passengers* (Cambridge, Mass.: MIT Press, 2022).
10. For the best single presentation of smooth space, see chapter 12 of Gilles Deleuze and Félix Guattari, *A Thousand Plateaus: Capitalism and Schizophrenia*, translated by Brian Massumi (Minneapolis: University of Minnesota Press, 1987).

2. PERIPHERAL POWER

1. In the first decade of the 2000s, there was an itinerant virtual exhibition mounted by the Science Museum of Minnesota. Plant movements were photographed and then sped up using the techniques of time-lapse photography. Children were then invited to dance "with" the plants, imitating their movements. For a glimpse of this wonderful experiment, see https://plantsinmotion.bio.indiana.edu/plantmotion/projects/plantdance/plantdance.html.
2. On the distinction between *inexact* and *anexact*, see Stephan Körner, *The Philosophy of Mathematics: An Introductory Essay* (London: Hassell Street, 2021). *Anexact* means not to be determinate by any recognized system of measurement.
3. An example of the indeterminacy of the place of plants is provided by professional gardener Morgan Cintron. He points out that in one single plot of a garden the receptivity of the soil—the same physically and chemically throughout—is differential from one area of the plot to another so that lavender plants will flourish in one part but not in another. Yet he cannot tell exactly where the line between hospitality

and inhospitality is to be drawn: it is intrinsically indeterminate so far as the receptivity to lavender is concerned. The exact dividing line is not subject to human measurement, not even that of an experienced gardener such as Cintron. Conversation with Morgan Cintron, June 15, 2022.

4. The same is true of ourselves as living bodies: our parts are more or less precisely configured, but our body as a whole is placed in its world in a radically indeterminate way. Suggested here is a deep link between embodied life and indeterminacy of place.

5. Alexander Pope, "An Epistle to Lord Burlington" (1731); his italics.

6. For an account of Darwin's claim—which has proven prescient—see Stefano Mancuso and Alessanda Viola, *Brilliant Green: The Surprising History and Science of Plant Intelligence* (Washington, D.C.: Island, 2015), pp. 132–36. The authors add that "in fact, the root tip is even more advanced than Darwin imagined, [it is] able to detect numerous physicochemical parameters in the environment" (p. 136). The same authors *pace* Darwin attribute special intelligence to the root tip—which is nothing if not a pointed edge.

7. For a description of this alternative spacing, see Edward S. Casey and Mary Watkins, *Up Against the Wall* (Austin: University of Texas Press, 2014), part 1, especially chapter 1.

8. For a more complete discussion of borders vs. boundaries, see Edward S. Casey, *The World on Edge* (Bloomington: Indiana University Press, 2017), chapter 1.

9. Edges that are *inexact* are such as may still be subject to precise measurement given the right circumstances of measurement and the employment of the right metric. *Anexact* edges, it will be recalled, characterize the place of plants as resistant to any and all precise determination.

10. To discourage such entry, the Border Patrol, while allowing the trees to stand, has inserted a series of locked metal doors that act to block traversal of this exceptional stretch of La Frontera. For a more complete description of this extraordinary situation, see Casey and Watkins, *Up Against the Wall*, pp. 97–99. At another location—at the University of Texas at Brownsville—the wall, which cuts across the campus, is festooned with flowers on trellis affixed to the wall itself

as if to gesture toward a receptivity that is otherwise excluded in the starkness of the wall in most of the rest of its serpentine length. For a more complete description, see Casey and Watkins, pp. 88–89.
11. See Derek Fell, *Cézanne's Garden* (New York: Simon and Schuster, 2003). His own garden was a condensation of this boundaried world, thanks to its dense vegetation and almost-hidden paths: "Cézanne's woodland garden is maintained by the present administration [of the estate] as a tapestry garden, to echo the visual drama of Cézanne's powerful garden and landscape paintings" (p. 71).

INTERLUDE I. HOW PLANTS THINK

1. Parmenides of Elea, "Fragments," in *Ancilla to the Presocratic Philosophers*, translated by Kathleen Freeman (Cambridge, Mass.: Harvard University Press, 1948), p. 42.
2. Hideyuki Takahashi and T. K. Scott, "Intensity of Hydrostimulation for the Induction of Root Hydrotropism and Its Sensing by the Root Cap," *Plant, Cell and Environment* 16 (1993): 99–103.
3. This insight has been watered down in the idea of philosophical mediations as the derivations of the middle.
4. This is a paraphrasing of Heidegger's diagnosis, "science itself does not think, and cannot think," in *What Is Called Thinking?* translated by Fred Wieck and J. Glenn Gray (New York: Harper and Row, 1968), p. 8.
5. Structures—above all, those of thinking—are in equal measure edified and strewn, scattered like seeds, in keeping with their Proto-Indo-European root *streu-*. Thus, with recourse to some overused terms from the past century, we might say that every structure is self-deconstructive.
6. Hannah Arendt, *Thinking Without a Banister: Essays in Understanding, 1953–1975*, edited by Jerome Kohn (New York: Schocken, 2018), p. 473.

3. TAKING TREES OVER THE EDGE

1. This chapter draws from Edward S. Casey and Michael Marder, "The Places of Trees," to appear in David Macauley, *The Wisdom of Trees:*

Thinking Through Arboreality, ed. David Macauley and Laura Pustarfi (Albany: State University of New York Press, forthcoming).
2. "In nature, the plant alone . . . is vertical, along with man" [L'arbre seul, dans la nature . . . est vertical, avec l'homme]," Paul Claudel, *La connaissance de l'Est* (Paris: Gallimard, 2000), p. 148.
3. Blaise Pascal, *Pensées*, translated and edited by Roger Ariew (Indianapolis: Hackett, 2004), p. 21.
4. We are reminded here of Leibniz's definition of matter as a garden within a garden within a garden, resulting in an infinity within something finite.
5. See Marjolein Oele, *E-Co-Affectivity* (New York: State University of New York Press, 2021).
6. See George Quasha's discussion of "ecoproprioception" in his *Poetry in Principle* (New York: Spuyten Duyvil, 2019), pp. 54–56, 72–73, 78; as well as a forthcoming article by the same title and authored by George Quasha in a special issue of *Ecosomatics* (2023).
7. For further on this sense of worlding in its sheer variety and with certain philosophical consequences, see Edward S. Casey, *The World on Edge* (Bloomington: Indiana University Press, 2017).

INTERLUDE 2. PLANTS UP-CLOSE: THE CASE OF MOSS

1. Jean-Jacques Rousseau, *Reveries of a Solitary Walker* (New York: Penguin, 1979), p. 84.
2. Francis Bacon, *Philosophical Works*, edited by James Spedding et al. (Boston: Brown and Taggard, 1862), 4:407. The expression is very telling, given especially the philosophical association of plants in toto with an imperfect (because immobile, insensitive, etc.) kind of life. Thus, for Bacon mosses and mushrooms are the most imperfect among all existing things.
3. Bacon, p. 406. *Excerned* means excreted, exuded through the pores.
4. Bacon, p. 405.
5. Hildegard von Bingen, *Physica*, translated by Priscilla Throop (Rochester, Vt.,: Healing Arts, 1998), p. 133.
6. Robin Wall Kimmerer, *Gathering Moss: A Natural and Cultural History of Mosses* (Corvallis: Oregon State University Press, 2003), p. 13.

7. Robert M. Stark, *A Popular History of British Mosses* (London: Lovell Reeve, 1852), p. 4.
8. Kimmerer, *Gathering Moss*, p. 5.
9. Kimmerer, p. 10.
10. "Musci," *The Edinburgh Encyclopaedia*, edited by David Brewster (Philadelphia: Joseph and Edward Parker, 1832), 14:2.
11. Rousseau, *Reveries of a Solitary Walker*, p. 118.
12. Friedrich Nietzsche, *Thus Spoke Zarathustra*, in *Portable Nietzsche*, edited by Walter Kaufmann (New York: Penguin, 1988), p. 135.

4. THE SHARED SOCIALITY OF TREES, WITH IMPLICATIONS FOR PLACE

1. For a more complete assessment of the power of the visual glance, see E. S. Casey, *The World at a Glance* (Bloomington: Indiana University Press, 2007).
2. Merlin Sheldrake, *Entangled Life: How Fungi Make Our Worlds, Change Our Minds, and Shape Our Futures* (New York: Random House, 2020), p. 12 and p. 19.
3. The story of Simard's coining of this term is told in her "Note from a Forest Scientist," in Peter Wohlleben, *The Hidden Life of Trees: What They Feel, How They Communicate* (New York: Random House, 2015), pp. 247–50.
4. Simard, pp. 248–49 (our italics).
5. Cited in Sheldrake, *Entangled Life*, p. 73.
6. Sheldrake, p. 91.
7. Simard, cited in Wohlleben, *The Hidden Life of Trees*, p. 249.
8. Wohlleben, p. 51 (in the chapter significantly titled "United We Stand, Divided We Fall").
9. Wohlleben, pp. 51–52. There is also the more specific scientific knowledge about just how communication happens. In particular, various biochemical substances are secreted both by the roots and by the aboveground portions of plants to communicate the approach of predators, drought conditions, underground sources of water, and so forth. In most cases, plant scientists do not know whether plants are communicating to other plants through such substances or to themselves (to their own distal parts), which are otherwise only loosely integrated

into the vegetal "whole." The term *eavesdropping* is used to describe how other plants pick up signals that, apparently, are intended for distal parts of the very plant that released them.
10. Wohlleben, p. 53.
11. Wohlleben, p. 51.
12. One of us (MM) has written several studies of attention in plants: see Michael Marder, "Plant Intelligence and Attention," *Plant Signaling and Behavior* 8, no. 5 (May 2013), e23902, and, more recently, Michael Marder, André Parise et al., "Do Plants Pay Attention? A Possible Phenomenological-Empirical Approach." *Progress in Biophysics and Molecular Biology* 173 (September 2022), 11–23, doi: 10.1016/j.pbiomolbio.2022.05.008.
13. Wohlleben, *The Hidden Life of Trees*, p. 17.
14. Wohlleben, p. 10.
15. See D. A. Perry, "A Moveable Feast: The Evolution of Resource Sharing in Plant-Fungus Communities," *Trends in Ecology and Evolution* 13 (1998): 432–34.
16. Michael Marder, "Plant Habitats," in Ute Meta Bauer, ed., *Climates. Habitats. Environments.* (Cambridge, Mass.: MIT Press, 2022), pp. 48–59.
17. Wohlleben, p. 17.
18. Tim Flannery, foreword to *The Hidden Life of Trees*, p. viii.
19. Flanery, p. viii (my italics).
20. Cited without attribution by Gary Snyder, "The Place, the Region, and the Commons," in *The Practice of the Wild* (Washington, D.C.: Shoemaker & Hoard, 1990), p. 33.
21. Snyder. These words are Snyder's.
22. Snyder, p. 39. Note that "natural contract" is also employed by Michel Serres and Bruno Latour.
23. Snyder, p. 41 (our italics).
24. "We are asking how the whole human race can regain self-determination in place after centuries of having been disenfranchised by hierarchy and/or centralized power" (p. 46).
25. A "biome" is definable as "a large naturally occurring community of flora and fauna occupying a major habitat, e.g., a forest or a tundra."
26. Snyder, "The Place, the Region, and the Commons," p. 44.
27. Snyder, p. 40.

28. See Mary Watkins, *Mutual Accompaniment and the Creation of the Commons* (New Haven: Yale University Press, 2019), especially chapter 10.
29. Watkins, p. 306.
30. A particularly perverse configuration of the commons then emerges in areas where monocultures are cultivated, disrespecting vegetal diversity, depleting the soil, and exposing all members of a plant community to greater dangers of fatal diseases, infestations, and toxic substances (released to prevent these on an ever-expanding scale).
31. See Watkins, *Mutual Accompaniment and the Creation of the Commons*, chapter 10: "Mutual Accompaniment and the Commons-to-Come."
32. Marjolein Oele, *E-Co-Affectivity: Exploring* Pathos *at Life's Material Interfaces* (Albany: State University of New York Press, 2021), p. 162. See the review of this book by Edward S. Casey, "Toward a Radically New Philosophical Ecology," *Research in Phenomenology* (forthcoming, 2024).
33. See Edward S. Casey, *Remembering: A Phenomenological Study*, 2nd ed. (Bloomington: Indiana University Press, 2009).
34. *Lot* is a specification of *plot*—one that takes into account dimensions and issues that we conventionally consider part of *real estate*: a term that connotes something settled or stable via the *sta-* root of "estate" and formally agreed-upon: *real* we can take as short for *realized*.
35. Sheldrake, *Entangled Life*, p. 91 (our italics).
36. Thich Nhat Hanh, *The Heart of Understanding* (Berkeley: Parallax, 1988), p. 4. See the entire chapter 4, "Interbeing."
37. See Richard Powers, *The Overstory* (New York: Norton, 2018).
38. Powers, p. 9.
39. Sheldrake, *Entangled Life*, pp. 82–83.
40. Sheldrake, pp. 82–83 (my italics).
41. See Michael Perlman, *The Power of Trees: The Reforesting of the Soul* (Dallas: Spring, 1994).

INTERLUDE 3. PLANTS FROM AFAR

1. Teresa Castro has written a number of insightful pieces on the relation between cinema and plants. Consult, in particular, Teresa Castro, "The Mediated Plant," *e-flux journal*, 102, September 2019,

https://www.e-flux.com/journal/102/283819/the-mediated-plant/. Giovanni Aloi has worked on reorienting the thinking about plants in visual art. Refer on this issue to his edited volume *Why Look at Plants?* (Leiden: Brill, 2019).
2. For a more complete discussion of the sublime in landscape painting, see Edward S. Casey, *Representing Place: Landscape Painting and Maps* (Minneapolis: University of Minnesota Press, 2002), chapter 2 ("Apocalyptic and Contemplative Sublimity") and chapter 4 ("Pursuing the Natural Sublime").

5. ATTACHMENT AND DETACHMENT IN THE PLACE OF PLANTS

1. On the intelligence of plants, especially as centered in roots, see Stefano Mancuso and Alessanda Viola, *Brilliant Green: The Surprising History and Science of Plant Intelligence* (Washington, D.C.: Island, 2015), pp. 129 ff., especially 136–46.
2. One of the authors (MM) has commented at length on the inversion of vegetal growth at the inception of Western metaphysics. In particular, in *Timaeus* 90a–b, Plato writes: "We declare that God has given to each of us, as his *daemon*, that kind of soul which is housed in the top of our body and which raises us—seeing that we are not an earthly but a heavenly plant—up from earth towards our kindred in the heaven. And herein we speak most truly; for it is by suspending our head and root from that region whence the substance of our soul first came that the divine power keeps upright our whole body" (*Timaeus* 90a–b). For a detailed interpretation of this passage, see chapter 1 in Michael Marder, *The Philosopher's Plant: An Intellectual Herbarium* (New York: Columbia University Press, 2014).
3. On ecoproprioception, see George Quasha, *Poetry in Principle* (New York: Spuyten Duyvil, 2019), pp. 67–84, and EC's discussion of this fecund concept in the foreword to this same book.
4. G. W. F. Hegel, *Philosophy of Nature: Encyclopedia of the Philosophical Sciences, Part II*, translated by A. V. Miller (Oxford: Oxford University Press, 2004), p. 344.
5. For more on this dynamic of vegetal passengerhood, see Michael Marder, *Philosophy for Passengers* (Cambridge, Mass. MIT Press, 2022).

6. A tumbleweed diaspore, which has already made a fleeting appearance in these pages, deviates from this rule, as virtually the entire plant detaches from the root to roam the earth in the wind. A perfect metaphor for an uprooted neoliberal individual, it invites a more direct comparison to human migrations than the scatter of pollen or seeds.
7. For more on the evolutionary dimension of this issue, see Tom de Jong and Peter Klinkhamer, *Evolutionary Ecology of Plant Reproductive Strategies* (Cambridge: Cambridge University Press, 2005).
8. Chris Arsenault, "Only 60 Years of Farming Left If Soil Degradation Continues," *Scientific American*, December 2014, https://www.scientificamerican.com/article/only-60-years-of-farming-left-if-soil-degradation-continues/.

CONCLUSION

1. Regarding the devastation of forests, see Jill Lepore, "The Control of Nature, Root and Branch: What We Owe to Trees," *New Yorker*, May 19, 2023, pp. 24–27.
2. Stefano Mancuso and Alessandra Viola, *Brilliant Green: The Surprising Hisotory and Science of Plant Intelligence* (Washington, D.C.: Island, 2015), p. 129.
3. Mancuso and Viola add: "every plant continuously registers a great number of environmental parameters (light, humidity, chemical gradients, the presence of other plants or animals, electromagnetic fields, gravity, and so on), and, on the basis of those data, has to make decisions regarding food, competition, defense, relations with other plants and animals—activity that is hard to imagine without resorting to the concept of intelligence!" (p. 131).
4. For this connection, consult chapter 1, "Plato's Plane Tree" in Michael Marder, *The Philosopher's Plant: An Intellectual Herbarium* (New York: Columbia University Press, 2014).
5. For more on this view of fire, see Michael Marder, *The Phoenix Complex: A Philosophy of Nature* (Cambridge, Mass.: MIT Press, 2023).

INDEX

arborescence, 53–54. *See also* ontology
Aristotle, xi, xiv, 39; and motion, 62; and place, 156; and plants, 145
artificial intelligence, 43; digitalization, 143
Attachment: and capitalism, 152; and detachment, 158; and place, 120, 122–23, 137–38, 143; plants and earth, 119–20, 122–24, 128–29. *See also* roots
attraction, 119, 122
attention, 115, 118, 166n12
Avicenna, 58

Bacon, Francis, 73–74, 78, 164n2
Bataille, Georges, 135
Bergson, Henri, 24, 54
Von Bingen, Hildegard, 74, 78
border, 33–36, 61; U.S.-Mexico, 34–36, 134
boundary, 34–37, 43; as indeterminate, 165; trees as, 61

branching: branches, 53; and edge, 59–60; and place, 50, 52; reaching out, 24, 53, 65–66, 100, 125; reaching up, 26–27, 49–50; and sociality, 148; visibility, 40, 121–22. *See also* directionality
Bridgeman, Charles, 30
Broadness, 154
Brown, Capability, 30
Burning Bush, 26–27

capitalism, 41, 48, 56, 135, 142–44, 152
care: arboreal care, 88, 92
Cézanne, Paul, 37, 163n11
Chernobyl, 136
children, 66, 71, 73, 78–79, 161n1
cinema and plants, 167n1
Claudel, Paul, 49
climate change, 11; and migration, 125; and plants, 136–38, 144; and place, 152
commons, 89–92; and capitalism, 142, 167n30

communication: and being-in-the-world, 95; and biochemistry, 100, 160n3, 165n9; between plants, 27, 43–44, 64, 82, 85–87. *See also* Heidegger, Martin; language
competition, 40, 93

Darwin, Charles, 31, 162n6
determinate, 20–21, 23; and borders, 35–36; and freedom, 44; overdetermination, 147; and photography, 105; and presence, 56; self-determination, 91; and site, 143. *See also* La Frontera; measure; metaphysics
deforestation, 12
Deleuze, Gilles, and Félix Guattari, xxii; middle, 66; rhizome, 49, 85; smooth space, 51, 161n10; striation, 15, 51, 54
democracy, 89. *See also* arboreal care
Derrida, Jacques, 135
Descartes, René, xvii, 39, 42, 44
detachment; and place, 131–32, 138; and plants, 129–32, 127; scholarly, 73–74
dialectic, xviii, 13–14, 23–24, 30, 104, 125, 129–30, 151. *See also* Hegel, G. W. F.
diaspora, 131–35, 137, 169n6
directionality, x, 8; and painting, 109, 111; and plant growth, 125–27, 134; and phenomenology, 65

drought, 27, 127. *See also* climate change
Dylan, Bob, 74

earth, 63; plant attachment to, 119–20, 122–24, 126, 128–29; regeneration of, 130
ecological resistance, 136
ecstatic, 23, 27, 43
edge, 19, 18–20, 24, 27, 32–33; and attachment, 125; and becoming, 37; and boundary, 34; and communication, 43; and decay, 33; as eventmental, 27–28, 31–32; and garden, 28–29, 58; as invitation, 28, 30; and the middle, 43; and painting, 113; and place, 23, 31–32, 69; and roots, 60; and site, 26; and teleology, 60; and time, 69; and trees, 48, 58–59, 61, 63–64. *See also* hospitality; language
etymology: community, 88; diaspora, 131; ecology, 103; place, 7, 59, 153–54; plant, 7, 8, 153–54; plot, 95; symbiosis, 84
eventmental, 57; edges as, 27–28, 31–32; and place, 9
experience, 107, 156; and landscape painting, 113, 116–17. *See also* Phenomenology

fate: of place, 145, 147–48, 150, 155; of plants, 147
Flannery, Tim, 88
freedom, viii, xi, 44, 130
La Frontera, 15, 33, 35

garden, ix, n164; British, 61, 127–28; and co-emplacement, 149; and edges, 28–29, 58; Príncipe Real Garden, 67; Stowe Gardens, 30; Versailles, ix, 28–30, 31, 61, 128
germination, 49, 69. *See also* diaspora; reproduction
Gibson, J. J., 112
glance: and landscape painting, 111–12; and plant attachment, 129
Glissant, Édouard, 134
gravitropism, 49
Group of Seven, 117
growth, 27, 53, 60, 64, 154; growth-thought, 39; and metaphysics, n168; neuron arborization, 44; and ontology, 152; sustainable growth, 41–42

Hegel, Georg Wilhem Friedrich, xviii–xixi, 79, 130, 135, 161n8; *Phenomenology of Spirit*, 12, 14
Heidegger, Martin, 13–14, 60, 88; being-in-the-world, 95
Heraclitus, 49
hierarchy, 75–76, 124–25; tacit ordering of plants, 127–28. *See also* line
hospitality, 161–62n3; arboreal hospitality, 82–85; and commons, 92–93, and ecology, 103; and garden, 30–31; and landscape painting, 117; and place, 55–56, 125
human life; and plants, 123–24, 129, 131–33
Husserl, Edmund, 60–61, 65, 97, 123

immanence, 47, 127, 156
indeterminacy, the indeterminate edge, 19–23, 32; and boundaries, 34–36, 156; and the human body, 162n4; and painting, 105, 107–8; and place, 105, 140–41, 161n3; and plant sex, 130
individuation, 54; and landscape painting, 113, 115; of trees, 67
intelligence: artificial, 43; of plants, 31, 123–24, 145, 159n2, 162n6
invasive species, 33

James, William, 128

Kant, Immanuel, 78, 112, 135, 168n2
Kimmerer, Robin Wall, 75

language, 6, 23, 70, 158; and painting 106; and place, 153, 155–56
Leibniz, G. W., 164n4
lichen, 85
line, 28–29, 30; axis, 50; and borders, 33, 35; de-lineation, 58. *See also* La Frontera
locomotion, viii, 57, 61–62
logic, 40, 50, 57, 57, 95; of arrival, 133; of investment and return, 135

Malebranche, Nicolas, 28
Mandela, Nelson, 1
measure, 140–45, 154
Merleau-Ponty, Maurice, 99, 113–14
metaphysical, 24, 152, n168; categories of identity, 24; determinate presence, 56; and moss, 73, 76

middle, xx, n163; and children, 66; and edge, 43; and hospitality, 82; Middle Passage, 134; and painting, 111; and plant thought, 40; and seed germination, 69; and voice, 130, 135

migration, 131–34, 137; migrants 33; refugees, 135–36. *See also* diaspora

Monet, Claude, 110–12, 115, 117

moss, 71, 72–76, 77–79; ancients on, 75; future growth, 75–76; and stagnation, 74-75, 79

mutation, 5, 22–23

mycelia, 86–88

Newton, Sir Isaac, 2

Nietzche, Friedrich, *Zarathustra*, 77–80

nomadism, 15–16, 51, 150

Le Nôtre, André, 28, 30, 61

Oele, Marijolein, 64, 93

ontology, 17, 52, 59, 85, 121, 152, 154, 156; and arborescence, 54; and attachment, 128–29; and being-in-place, vii, 41, 57, 62–63, 69–70, 95, 96, 98, 156; becoming, 37, 53–54, 107; and flattening, 59, 153–55; here-and-there, 11–14, 141–42, 155; interbeing, 99–104; and movement, 75; species-being, 45; subjectivity, 114, 116. *See also* Hegel, G. W. F; Heidegger, Martin

orientation, xii, 12

painting, background, 111, 114, 118, 119; close-up, 112; landscape, 109–14, 116–17; and plants in place, 105–9, 111, 113–14, 116–17; realist painting, 106–7, 113; and returnability, 116, 156; and spectacle, 110–12, 113, 117–18

paradox, 6–8; and edges, 23; and here-and-there, 142; and middle, 40–41; and painting plants, 105, 114; and place of plants, 152–53; and trees, 86. *See also* Hegel, G. W. F

Parmenides, 39

Pascal, Blaise, 55

perception, 60–61; and landscape, 112–14; multisensory, 126, 128–29; of a presentation, 110

peripatetic, xi, xii; phyto-peripatetics, vii

periphery, 3, 18–23, 31; periphenomenological, xiii. *See* edge

Perlman, Michael, 103

phenomenology, 5, 12, 14, 16, 65; and migration, 134; phytophenomenology, 5; of trees, 47, 50, 59–60; of the vegetal, 13, 18, 22, 23, 39, 57–58

physiology, 27, 49, 64

Pierce, Charles Sanders, 105

place: 2, 5–6, 16, 40, 44, 47–54, 147, 150, 156; attachment to, 119–23, 128–29, 137–38, 149; and being, 53–54, 62–63, 69–70, 91, 150, 154–55; and being-in-the-world, 6, 96, 99, 130; and capitalism, 152; and climate change, 152; and commons, 89–92; and detachment, 133, 138; as determinate, 91; and diaspora, 131–133, 135; as dynamic, 9–11 150–151, 154; and ecoproprioception, 143; and edges, 19–23, 31–33, 48, 61; and egoism, 55; etymology of, 7, 95, 153–154; as eventmental, 57; fate of, 145, 147–48, 150, 155; flattening of, 155; as here-and-there, 11–14, 141–42, 148; and home, 11; and hospitality, 30–31, 55; as indeterminate, 108, 140–41, 156, 161n3; language of, 140, 153, 155–56; and measurability, 95, 140–45; and migration, 33, 131–36; and nomadism, 15–16, 51, 150; and ontology, 52, 154, 156; and painting, 107–9, 111, 114, 116, 118; paradox of, 40–41, 105, 152–53; and placelessness, 135–38, 146; as a presentational scene, 7–9; returning to, 116–17, 156; and roots, 95, 119–24, 129, 154; and site, 22, 48, 142–43; as a theatrical stage, 154; and trees, 47–48, 49–53, 55–57, 61, 67–70, 95–97; and visibility, 121. *See also* diaspora; Hegel, G. W. F; Heidegger, Martin; Quasha, George

plant blindness, 119

plant thinking, 39–40, 43; and artificial intelligence, 43
Plato, xv, 55, 76; Platonic Ideas, 124–25, 146; and trees, 153
Pope, Alexander, 31
Powers, Richard, 101
presentation: and plant attachment, 126, 128–29; and landscape painting, 110, 112, 117
property, 58, 90, 95. *See* capitalism

Quasha, George, 64, 128–29, 143

reproduction, 42; plant birth, 129; plant sex, 130–32, 134; soil fertility, 137
roots, 24, 52–53, 66, 68, 131, 137, 154, 163n2; and art, 108, 111; and communication, 85; and edges, 60; and intelligence, 31, 40, 123–24; as invisible, 119–21, 124, 148; as lived-body, 99–100; and place, 95, 129; rooting down, 26, 49–50; rootless, 74
Rousseau, Jean-Jaques, x, xi, n159; on moss, 72–73, 77–79

Schiller, Friedrich, 135
sessility, x, 2, 4, 24, 47, 141;and attachment, 122; burning bush, 27; and phenomenology, 13–14; and place, 150, 160n2; and plants, 17, 64, 74–75
Shakespeare, William, 61
Sheldrake, Merlin, 83–85, 89, 91, 99, 102, 148
Simard, Suzanne, 83, 86

site; and branching, 52; and capitalism, 143; collapsing into place, 22, 142–43; as distinguished from space and place, 57; and measurability, 48, 52–54

sociality, 56, n160; arboreal, 81, 83–84, 100–1, 148; and fungi, 83–88. *See also* communication

solar, 26–27, 55

Skeat, Walter, 7

Snyder, Gary, xiii–xiv, xvi, 94; and commons, 90

Socrates, 23

Soilocene, 93. *See also* Oele, Marjolein

space; and migration, 134; and nomadism, 51; and organic phenomena, 54–55; and painting, 113; and plants, 141; and place, 55, 57; smooth space, 161n10; and trees, 96. *See also* Deleuze, Gilles, and Félix Guattari

spectacle. *See* painting

symbiosis, 84, 141

Tagus River, 34

teleology, 60

theatrical stage, 154

time, viii, 12; and arborescence, 53–54; and capitalism, 143; and detachment, 137; and edge, 69; and migration, 134; and moss, 76–77; and organic phenomena, 54–55; and painting, 107–8; and place, 57, 62; and plant growth, 42;

touch; and communication, 85, 100; and edge, 26; and immediacy, 109; and moss, 71; and painting, 106, 113–14; and vision, 18–19. *See also* phenomenology; Treaty of Guadalupe Hidalgo, 34

United Nations, 137

vegetal communism, 88, 90

vegetal heteronomy, 135. *See also* ontology

vegetal wager, 135

Versailles, ix, 28–30, 31, 61, 128

vision; and landscape painting, 116; ocularcentrism, 18, 120–21; and ordering, 127, 129; plant visibility, 121–22, 139

vitality, 43, 73–74; and edge, 26; *élan vital*, 24; and middle, 69; and place of plants, 39, 150. *See also* Bergson, Henri

walking, viii, ix, xi, xv, 44, 115–16

Watkins, Mary, xv, 91–92

Wohlleben, Peter, 86–88, 91

Xenophanes, 50

zero-sum, 56

Printed and bound by CPI Group (UK) Ltd, Croydon, CR0 4YY
28/05/2024

14507558-0001